Writing Workouts to Develop Common Core Writing Skills

Writing Workouts to Develop Common Core Writing Skills

Step-by-Step Exercises, Activities, and
Tips for Student Success, Grades 2–6

Kendall Haven

 LIBRARIES UNLIMITED

AN IMPRINT OF ABC-CLIO, LLC
Santa Barbara, California • Denver, Colorado • Oxford, England

Library of Congress Cataloging-in-Publication Data

Haven, Kendall F.
 Writing workouts to develop Common Core writing skills : step-by-step exercises, activities, and tips for student success, grades 2–6 / Kendall Haven.
     pages cm
  Includes bibliographical references and index.
   ISBN 978–1–61069–866–5 (pbk.) — ISBN 978–1–61069–867–2 (ebook) 1. English language—Composition and exercises—Study and teaching (Elementary) I. Title.
 LB1576.H3238   2015
 372.62′3—dc23   2014027059

ISBN: 978–1–61069–866–5
EISBN: 978–1–61069–867–2

19 18 17 16 15   1 2 3 4 5

This book is also available on the World Wide Web as an eBook.
Visit www.abc-clio.com for details.

Libraries Unlimited
An Imprint of ABC-CLIO, LLC

ABC-CLIO, LLC
130 Cremona Drive, P.O. Box 1911
Santa Barbara, California 93116-1911

This book is printed on acid-free paper ∞

Manufactured in the United States of America

*This book is dedicated to
the students
of the Franklin Unified School District
who helped me refine and test
a number of these activities.*

CONTENTS

INTRODUCTION

Why learn to write? Writing is hard. Teaching writing devours large chunks of classroom time in every grade beginning in 1st. Blocks of time each day are devoted to spelling, to grammar, to vocabulary, and to other mechanical aspects of writing. Precious little time can be squeezed from the remains of each day's mandates to work on teaching students how to effectively and powerfully communicate when they write. That is, to plan, draft, evaluate, revise, and edit whatever content they want to (or have been assigned to) write. It is a legitimate question to ask: why bother? Why dedicate so much time to writing?

Learning to write should never be viewed as an end goal in and of itself. Rather, writing is a means to a goal (effective communication). "Writing" doesn't mean "learn-the-symbols-and-write-them-down." It means "convince, persuade, inspire, entertain, and teach through your writing as effectively as you would through conversation if you and the reader sat next to each other on the sofa." This book provides a variety of tested writing activities that can guide students to that level of writing competency.

GOAL

The new common core standards require that students develop the ability to write beyond spelling and forming a sentence. They must translate mental images, ideas, and emotions into written language that successfully transfers those ideas, images, and emotions to another person. Beyond the mechanical skills of spelling, grammar, sentence structure, punctuation, and vocabulary lie the writing skills that allow the writer to powerfully and effectively *communicate*—ideas, concepts, images. Those are the writing skills that this book is designed to develop. You want your students to comfortably possess the writing know-how to effectively communicate whatever they want to get across on paper. This book will help.

The obvious goal of a writing book is to build basic writing skill, muscle, and confidence. However, equally important, successful writing programs develop a positive writing attitude in students. Teachers and librarians need to build writing *enthusiasm* as well as writing ability. Without a modicum of enthusiasm for writing, any skill improvement will quickly atrophy from lack of use and practice.

That writing is an important skill is not debated or questioned. Research also shows that mastery of writing process links to general education success and to students' analytical, logical, and general mental development. After several years of study, the College Board test creators released the following statement in mid-2010: "Of all the sections of the SAT, the writing section is the most predictive of college success." Through two earlier studies of my own, I have been able to establish a direct, positive link between writing skill development and improved reading comprehension. Learning to effectively write seems to be a "gateway" precursor to mastery of other academic subjects or skill sets.

Reasonably rapid, effective writing is a basic 21st-century life skill, as well as an academic skill of increasing importance under the demands of the common core standards and standardized testing. One goal of this book is to provide writing activities that help each teacher squeeze as much writing proficiency development out of each available minute as possible. Once developed, these core writing skills allow students to readily respond to a variety of prompts and writing response styles. This book will arm librarians and teachers with tools, proven activities, and research-based concepts that will allow them to better guide their students toward successful writing proficiency.

WHAT MAKES WRITING HARD?

If writing is so important to student general development, why, then, is it consistently so hard for students to master writing? Why is writing so much harder than talking? Setting aside the mechanical challenges of writing (holding a pen, placing fingers on a keyboard, having thumbs blur across a cell phone keypad), the wiring and structure of the human brain hold important evolutionary answers.

Humans have been speaking for over 1,000,000 years. We can document that they were telling stories to each other several hundred thousand years ago. Because of this long dependence on speech, the human brain now has dedicated regions (especially Broca's and Wrenicke's areas and those sub-regions surrounding the Sylvian fissure) dedicated to processing language and speech. Children learn to speak all on their own because their brains are wired to emphasize and to develop that ability.

Not so with writing and reading. Writing (like reading) is a new human activity. Sumerian—generally agreed to be the first written language—is no more than 7,000 years old. At the time of the American Revolution, far less than half of the American population was literate. In the long history of humanoids on this planet, we have been reading and writing *en masse* for only the tiniest fraction of time.

There is no brain center for writing. Our DNA carries no genes for writing or reading. There may be in another 100,000 years. But not now. Lacking any dedicated brain space, learning to read and write must steal space from other brain areas as those processes are taught and learned. Speaking is naturally and automatically learned by each individual. Writing, like reading, is not.

The tools and activity of writing must be systematically taught. It requires engaging activities that stretch skills while holding the attention and focus of students. Enter this book with its series of powerful and proven tips and writing activities. I have crafted these workout activities by combining my in-class experience in over 3,000 schools and over 12,000 individual classrooms (the practical what-*really*-works? experience) with extensive research into story structure and the cognitive effects of individual story elements to produce the activities included here.

I have in-class tested each of these activities multiple times in multiple schools in multiple states—many used over 100 times at each of the recommended grade levels. These work. They are time efficient. They develop the essential writing muscle to apply to a variety of writing tasks and prompts listed on standardized writing assignments in virtually every state.

Writing skills can be broken into two distinct groups of skills that are typically presented in separate blocks—or periods—of instruction in American schools.

- **Mechanical skills**: spelling, grammar, sentence structure, punctuation, capitalization, and vocabulary
- **Content skills:** planning, researching, drafting, evaluating, revising, and editing the material to be written

This book focuses primarily on the ***content*** aspects of writing since virtually every school language arts textbook focuses primarily (and often almost exclusively) on the mechanical aspects of writing. I will touch on mechanical concerns only in the section on editing.

PREVIOUS WRITING BOOKS

Available research conclusively shows that story structure underlies successful formation of the "thing" to be communicated if that "thing" is to be compelling and effective. That notion was the basis for my book *Story Proof* and my new follow-on book, *Story Smart*. Those books focus not on the process of communicating something to an audience or reader, but on how to organize and structure the information you want to communicate—and on the neural and cognitive science that explains the power and effectiveness of what we commonly call "effective story structure." Those two books do not deal directly with the act of communicating, but with creating and planning the structural architecture to later be communicated.

Story Proof and *Story Smart* collectively provide the research basis for centering the planning and development process around the Eight Essential Elements of effective story structure. My Libraries Unlimited books *Get It Write!* and *Write Right!* provide (combined) over 100 games and activities to teach that structure and those informational elements to students. Collectively, those books address the writer's planning process. That is, they guide students into the habit of planning and creating effective material to communicate before they begin to actually write (or speak).

Get It Write! is about exercising individual elements of effective story structure (like practicing individual instruments of an orchestra). This book is about writing flowing music for the orchestra as a whole once you know what the individual instruments each can do to contribute to the overall musical sound you want to create. To do that, we will focus on honing the skills of writing in conjunction with the skills of creating.

USING THIS BOOK

All TIPs and workouts of the book link to core curriculum elements and to state language arts standards for virtually every state. However, this book is not designed to serve as a formal language arts textbook. Rather, it will serve as a comprehensive, proven guide with in-class tested activities to arm teachers and school librarians with the approaches, knowledge, and activities to meet their students' needs and to teach and inspire their students to write.

I have collected solid research-based underpinnings for all concepts and techniques to be included. However, I do not intend to focus on a presentation of research. Rather, I will focus on the practical application of tested research concepts. I have personally, and repeatedly, tested every activity to be included in the book and will rely heavily on that personal in-class experience and results in presenting detailed directions for the use of these materials.

I have designed the concepts and assignments to be fun as well as instructive—fun both for teacher and for students. I have successfully used every activity I include, and have gotten positive teacher and student feedback on each. The range of included activities will make students *want* to write. Only then can teachers effectively teach them *how* to write.

The book is also conceived to work within the realities of modern schools and classrooms. This will be a practical guide that will efficiently—as well as effectively—improve student writing performance within the fierce constraints and realities under which librarians and teachers must function.

I have divided the workouts into three groups based on the grade levels where I have found the greatest success with that activity: Primary, Intermediate, and those workouts that work wonderfully well across the 2nd-grade through 6th-grade range. And, yes, there are many that do.

Beyond that ordering from (in general) youngest to older, is there any significance to the order of individual workouts? Answer: no. Feel free to jump around and use those that fit with the flow of your classroom teaching. Every workout in this book has consistently created both writing enthusiasm and significantly improved writing skill.

You will notice that I regularly include time for students to share their work and for the class to discuss those shared submissions. I have observed that there is great value and benefit in having students hear what other students did with the same assignment. It provides a time for reflection and mental revision. It provides tested models of writing for students to emulate in the future. Enjoy!

THE WRITER'S TOOLBOX

Every carpenter drags a personal box of tools to each jobsite. That toolbox contains all of the essential tools and supplies the carpenter needs in order to get the assigned job done. But that carpenter also drags a mental toolbox to the jobsite that contains his/her accumulated knowledge of how to effectively use each tool.

Similarly, each writer is armed with both a physical and a mental writing toolbox that he hauls around to each writing assignment. While the writer's physical toolbox (vocabulary, spelling, grammar, punctuation, penmanship, etc.) is both real and important, it is his mental toolbox—his experience of writing concepts and techniques that will allow that writer to combine, mold, maneuver, and manipulate words to successfully communicate—that is most important and also the focus of this book.

How does a writer create suspense and excitement? Or create and develop interesting characters? Or build the tension around a climax? Or grab readers with an opening hook? Or create consistently vivid and compelling imagery? Or build a convincing and persuasive case for their ideas? Or draw readers into a story so that they vicariously experience the story events? These are some of the writing tools student writers can develop through these workouts and tuck away in their mental writer's toolbox.

A NOD TO FLUENCY

Fluency is a measure of how fast a student can write. Amazingly, that simple measure consistently ranks as the best mechanical predictor of the *quality* of future writing content and general writing success. Apparently, it's frustrating to have to slow your mind to match the snail-like speed of your hand. Minds that have to continuously stomp on their mental brakes to retard racing mental creativity don't seem able to create nearly as effectively.

Research also shows that fluency (along with a conscious knowledge of effective story structure) is one of the major building blocks of students' initial attitude toward writing. Fluency is a relatively easy skill to bolster in early grades. Yet, even though it appears to be critical to writing success, most school primary grade curricula give, at best, a passing nod to this activity, and many completely ignore it.

Want to check the fluency of your students? Give each student a set text to copy. You can project the text on a central screen, but that forces students to repeatedly look up and down, up and down, thus artificially depressing all fluency scores. Better to hand each student a page with the prescribed text and then see how many words each student can copy over the course of one minute. That's fluency.

Fluency is not a measure of a child's ability to create. However, success with this early physical element of writing seems to spill over to strongly influence both attitude toward writing and, therefore, the amount of effort and energy a child expends on writing.

There are a number of good books and websites devoted to fluency. I recommend that you check them out.

CHAPTER 1

THE FIVE STEPS OF SUCCESSFUL WRITING

Ask your class, "What makes a good writer?" and let them discuss and develop their collective answer. I have asked this question of many students, but also of groups of professional storytellers and story writers.

Many answer that "some have the gift, and most of us don't." That is—in my opinion— both wrong and overly simplistic. Certainly, natural writing ability is distributed among us humans on a normal distribution curve. (You know that classic distribution curve—technically a Poisson distribution—that tapers off smoothly and evenly at both ends and with a great hump in the middle.) Running ability, artistic talent, singing, cooking, fiddle playing, mechanical drawing, and every other specific skill seem to be distributed according to the same pattern.

Some naturally are given greater writing ability. True enough. But that begs the question: what makes a good writer? That is, can *any* student, starting with whatever natural writing talent they possess, become a sufficiently "good" writer to be consistently *effective* in their writing? And what does it take for him or her to do so?

That's the real question. After much observation and thought, here is my six-part answer.

1. Be curious, observe. Probe. Pose questions. Explore. Be easily fascinated. Peer beyond the surface of things, people, and ideas. Treat everything as if it were a mechanical clock begging to be disassembled—just so you can see how it works.

2. Master story structure. (The Eight Essential Elements. See TIP #5.) These eight elements reflect how the reader's brain is hardwired to make sense out of what they read. Master those eight elements and you make it easy for readers to understand and make sense from what you write. I have written several books on these elements and the process of using them.

3. Read—often and critically. Enjoy reading. But also critically analyze what the writer did—both when you enjoyed the writing and when you didn't. How did he get you to see images of his story? How did he get you to feel different emotions? How did he structure his sentences and paragraphs? Etc.

4. Write. The more you do it, the better you get. Also, critically evaluate your own writing. Don't beat yourself up, but honestly decide what worked as you hoped it would and how you would write it differently next time.

5. Always be willing to revise and edit. ("I *will* remember the 1st rule of writing: No one gets it right on the 1st draft." See TIP #2.)

6. Master the mechanics of writing. These are the technical tools of the trade. Every painter needs to master brushstrokes. Every dancer spends hours holding onto a bar practicing basic positions and single moves. These are the fundamental tools artists use to express themselves. And, yes, writing is an art; and, yes, you need to master those basic mechanical tools of writing.

That said, effective writing isn't a single process. In fact, it is the end result of five separate steps, each with its own concerns, goals, focus, pace, and techniques. In order to produce a final well-written product, the writer must plan, draft, evaluate, revise, and edit.

Step 1. Planning

Planning is all about ... well, planning. It is the step when you take the time to create and to explore. Let your imagination soar. Use what-ifs. Think about each of the Eight Essential Elements. Try on different ideas like you'd try on different clothes at the store before you bought any.

Create first; write second. (See TIP #1.) That is the first rule of writing; the research is quite clear on this. Anyone for whom the mechanical act of writing is a conscious effort—i.e., virtually all students—can't successfully create and write at the same time. That part of the brain responsible for the mechanical acts of writing (holding pencil, fingers on keyboard, forming letters, picking the right letters, forming a sentence, etc.) has the ability to shut down the creative part of the brain. The reverse is not true. When they try to do both together (as virtually all students do), creativity falters. What is created tends to be bland, simple, plot-driven, and ... well, boring.

Create first, and only write once the thing you create is worth writing. Talk it, talk about it, draw it, act it, doodle it. **Play** with what you are going to write, and then write. If, on timed writing assessments, students allotted 20 percent of their available time to this planning process, they would make the actual writing both far easier and far more coherent and effective.

My previous writing books *Get It Write!* and *Write Right!* also focus on this planning process and on developing the tools and habits that make for effective writers.

In this book I will extend the process to the development of more comprehensive tools for each student writer's toolbox—techniques to master and to (yes!) enjoy.

Step 2. Drafting

Planning is when the writer builds up a reservoir of ideas and details—like piling water into a lake behind a dam. Drafting is the time to throw open the floodgates. Let the pent-up ideas gush out. This is the time to let the words fly. Write with abandon, with passion, with emotion! Drafting is the time for a "data dump," from mind to paper, a time to get all of your thoughts down on paper for the first time. Drafting is a time for letting the vivid details and emotions flow.

Go for the conflict. Make it exciting! If you don't do those things during drafting, they are ever-so-much harder to install later.

Don't stop to edit, to spell check, to worry about grammar or capitalization, or to correct wording. There will be plenty of time for those activities later. During draft writing, keep writing. No, there is no need to draft an entire story, article, or report all at once. Break it into logical chunks (section, chapter, scene), and draft those individually once you are ready with the images and details for that part of the whole. Then stop and prep for the next part you'll draft. Put it together and smooth it out after you have written each individual part.

Don't worry if you don't know exactly where to begin. First-draft beginnings are always wrong and need to be changed and revised later. So don't worry about it. Dive in and start, knowing full well that it will be easy to fix it once you see the entire story on paper.

First drafts are always lousy. Still, they are a critically important step in the process. Plan as best you can. Then trust yourself and write! No, not all experienced writers write this way. But it is my experience in working with students that it is by far the best writing plan for beginning writers.

Step 3. Evaluate

Evaluation is that step most teachers and students overlook. It's the step there is never enough time to formally include in student writing efforts. Evaluation is that step wherein a writer decides exactly what needs to be revised and edited—and what does not. Often, after formal evaluation, small and simple changes can make huge—and extremely satisfying—improvements in the success of the piece.

Far too many student writers, however, finish drafting and instantly dive into editing. Don't do it. Write it and set it aside. Then come back and evaluate the writing. What works? Where do you need to add paragraphs or scenes? Where do you need to cut? Are the characters interesting and well developed? Are the Eight Elements all there? Did you begin at the best spot? Does each scene have sufficient details? Are the opening, climax, and resolution all satisfying? Will the reader easily follow the flow of the main character's struggles?

I included a large section on evaluation in my book *Write Right!* and refer you to that book for detailed ideas for both self-evaluation and peer-evaluation techniques.

It is immensely difficult for writers to evaluate their own writing. Why? They already know exactly what they wanted to say. They already hold detailed images of each scene and point in their minds. Thus, *any* words on the page will pop those already-existing images back into their head—and those images are perfect! Many student writers conclude that, therefore, the words they wrote must also be perfect—or at least completely adequate.

A writer cannot accurately evaluate what he writes until all of the images have dissipated that he formed in his mind in order to write. Research says that, for most people, that takes several weeks. However, classrooms rarely afford that time luxury. The alternative is to provide a structured process—an evaluation checklist—for students to use either for author evaluations or for peer evaluations.

Remember: you can't fix it until you decide exactly what needs to be fixed. If you have a leak in a plumbing system, you don't attack the problem by randomly changing pieces of pipe. No. First you evaluate. You find out exactly what leaks and only change out those parts. Same with writing.

First drafts are always lousy. Good writers always take the time to make them better. That begins not with revision and editing, but with evaluation.

Do you have to take the time for this step on every student writing effort? Absolutely not. However, students should include it often enough to understand *how* to evaluate their writing, what evaluation does for their writing, and the impact on the quality of their final written product when there isn't sufficient time for this step.

Step 4. Revise

"Revise" and "edit" are separate steps. Every teacher wants students to edit. Every student knows about (and usually loathes) editing. No one pays much attention to revision. It, like evaluation, is an often overlooked step that can fix many problems with a draft that editing cannot touch.

Publishers often call editing "line editing" because you go over every line, and every word. Not so during revision. Here we play with big hunks of the story: move scenes, add scenes, reorder the scenes, build tension through the first half of the story, decide if the climax works or if you need to build that scene, rewrite the opening to better hook and grab readers, revise the character description for one character that you have sprinkled throughout the story so that readers get a stronger emotional reaction to him/her, sprinkle more humor throughout . . . that sort of thing.

It is important to revise *before* editing. Why? Because I have observed that, once students struggle to find just the right adjective for one sentence, or just the right bit of sensory detail, then they will never—NEVER—be willing to cut it, even if they later decide that that entire paragraph should go. They would much prefer to leave that precious detail in, even if it kills the story and ruins their grade.

While revising, a writer will already often chop out multiple paragraphs and decide to completely rewrite others. Anyone committed to a sprinkling of precious details will never be willing to do the hard work of sending them to the trash heap. (In writing circles, it's called "Kill Your Darlings.")

Often, the only way to build in time (especially your time as well as student writing time) for a real couple of rounds of revision is to do it on things students write for core curriculum subjects (reports on the stars, on explorers, on social studies topics, etc.).

Step 5. Edit

Editing is all about precision, the process of making sure that every word, phrase, sentence, and paragraph conveys exactly what you intended for them to convey. Once the story is set in place, it's time to focus on the details, on individual words. Editing is the great time sink of writing. By most estimates, easily 90 percent of the time professional writers spend writing, they spend editing. Editing is like polishing. You can't polish your way to a great marble statue. The statue has to be carved, shaped, and molded in the previous steps. Polishing then brings out its greatest glowing luster. Polishing makes the piece look as luminous and breathtaking as possible. Wood-carvers and stonemasons never actually finish polishing. They just keep at it until the piece is taken away.

Same with writing.

Writers examine every sentence, phrase, word, and detail—and the images they create. Can I find a better word that is more interesting, more descriptive, more powerful, more efficient, more unusual, more "grabbing"? Start to finish. Top to bottom. Then you start over and do it again, searching for yet better words, descriptions, and images.

Once the words are set, then, on one last edit run-through, check spelling. No need to check spelling until you're sure you are going to keep the words you check.

There are many decent guides to editing for students. I included a detailed section on it in my book *Write Right!* and refer you to that book for editing checklists and progressions.

DO YOU HAVE TO DO THEM ALL?

Teachers are forever pressed for time. Many express the frustration that they don't even have adequate time to teach minimal proficiency in the mechanical skills of writing, and certainly don't have time (either their own out-of-class time or student in-class time) to extend each writing project through extensive planning, evaluation, revision, and editing.

The questions arise: if I can't do them all, is there any point in doing anything beyond a single student draft with quick mechanical editing correction? Which of the other steps are the most important? The least important? If I don't have very much time, which step(s) will prove most productive?

Here is my advice. Each of those steps is a valuable—even necessary—part of an effective writing package. However, that doesn't mean that you must include time for them all on every writing activity. For each student writing effort, decide what you want your students to focus on for that particular bit of writing.

If, for example, you opt to skip evaluation and revision, and to limit editing to one quick pass to correct mechanical errors (spelling, grammar, and capitalization), that's fine. However, you should tell students the steps you expect them to do and which they (for this assignment) should skip. That places this writing within the greater context of the complete writing process. I recommend that you also briefly discuss with students how those omitted steps are likely to impact the quality of their final product.

Having said that, I also believe that emerging student writers gain more from an emphasis on different steps at different grade levels. I would assign the steps (other than drafting—something that is always done) in this order of importance for student writing development.

1. **Planning.** Effective pre-writing planning is the most productive habit students can develop. It applies to the writing at all grade levels from first grade through graduate school.

   Without a bit of time devoted just to planning, there is little point in seriously going further. Planning doesn't require great amounts of time. A good guideline is to set aside 20 percent of total available time for planning. (Certainly, the ideal percentage will vary from student to student.) Don't worry that planning time will significantly cut into either the quantity or the quality of what students write on timed assessments. Most students find that in the remaining 80 percent they get more written, and that that writing is far better, than they would have if they had begun to write immediately.

2. **Evaluation.** Even if students do no revision or editing, it is extremely valuable to thoughtfully evaluate each piece of writing. That's how they learn. That's how they improve. I find that developing evaluation skills becomes relevant and productive beginning with the intermediate grades and develops in sophistication and depth up through high school.

3. **Editing.** Learning how to quickly and efficiently manipulate words, images, and sentences in order to effectively communicate is a critical life skill. Everyone needs to be able to do it. The best time to develop that skill is when editing your own writing. Mechanical skill editing can begin as soon as students produce written work. However, I find that content editing (details, sensory images, strong action verbs, character development, etc.) doesn't really take hold for most students until around 4th grade.

4. **Revision**. Revision is an amazingly powerful and effective writing tool. At some point, every writer must grit their teeth and learn to do it. However, I find that students do best by mastering the other steps first. This slides revision, as a writing skill, into the realm of high school. By that time, student writing skills should have advanced to a point where they can both understand the need for specific revisions to what they write and envision the effect of possible revision schemes.

CHAPTER 2

WRITING TIPS

I visit classrooms and work with students and teachers all across the country. And I notice people driving into the same writing potholes and detouring down the same dead ends everywhere. Time after time, I notice that students stumble in the same writing spots because of the same misconceptions.

I have distilled more than a "baker's dozen" writing road signs designed to help you and your students avoid those pesky writing traps into a series of TIPS. They will serve you and your students well. Recite them; chant them; write them on the wall. It would be wonderful if all 13 tips popped into students' minds whenever they think of writing.

TIP #1. CREATE FIRST; WRITE SECOND

Research has shown that few can create and write at the same time. This is especially true for those for whom the mechanical act of writing (holding a pencil, forming letters, spelling, fluency, grammar, etc.) is at all a conscious effort. This probably includes virtually all of your students. When they try to do both together (write as they create the content they will write), they stop creating. Their content is typically uninspired, plodding, and . . . well . . . boring.

How to get around this deadly dilemma? Create first; write second. That is, don't start actually writing a narrative text until it has been planned and developed.

Try this quick demo if you doubt how deeply ingrained this write-right-away habit is. Tell your students to take out a piece of paper and get a sharpened pencil. Tell them they will have five minutes to write. Then give them a topic like "What this school needs most," or "If I ran the school," or "The class field trip I'd most like for us to take." That sort of personal opinion essay topic.

Then say "Go!" (or "Begin") and carefully watch. My experience is that 9 out of 10 students will immediately begin to write. Most of that final 10th never get around to writing anything unless you stand glaring over their shoulder. The point is, almost all of your students just did the one thing that best guarantees lack of success in their writing. They began to write, hoping that something worth writing would appear while they wrote. Unfortunately, more often than not, it won't.

When you plan, create the Eight Essential Elements that define an effective story (see my other writing books or TIP #5, below). When planning, draw it, talk it, act it, doodle it, even jot down a few notes and key words. These activities don't impede the creative process. Writing *does*. I have developed and described dozens of prewriting activities to help students find and develop their stories before they begin the first draft.

Students counter that they are terrified that they'll forget what they create if they don't write it down as they create it. I have tested this notion in hundreds of classrooms. In almost all cases, what they actually do forget was worth forgetting. What's worth remembering, they will remember if they create strong, vivid images for it as they create and plan and talk through the piece they want to write. The best solution for this "I'll forget" fear is a tape recorder. (See TIP #6.)

Then when you write, focus on the details—on selecting strong action verbs, on including powerful descriptive language.

I have also often heard that students feel squeezed for time on timed writing assessments and fear that if they don't start writing right away, they'll never finish. I have tested this notion as well. If students take the time to plan, they then write faster and more succinctly. They will actually finish in less time—and the quality of their writing will rise significantly.

Best rule of thumb: allow 20 percent of available time for planning, 80 percent for writing. Create first; write second.

TIP #2. FIRST DRAFTS ARE ALWAYS LOUSY

No one gets it right the first time. No one. Every successful writer must revise and edit. Some very successful writers rewrite each page as many as 50 times! If your students write mediocre—even lousy—first drafts, don't (D-O—-N-O-T) allow them to think that this means they are lousy writers. It just means that they are just like everybody else: they write mediocre to lousy first drafts.

First drafts are just that . . . first drafts. Writing is rewriting. First drafts represent the process of dumping all of your thoughts down on paper for the first time. If you have planned well (pre-drafting creative activities), that first draft will be much more coherent and will flow better. But it will still be just a first draft and will still need serious revision, editing, and polishing if it is to shine with its greatest potential.

Many students claim to write perfectly acceptable—even "good"—first drafts (and thereby claim that their writing disproves this important tip). I always respond that even a *seemingly* good first draft pales in comparison to how wonderful the writing will be after several rounds of revision and editing. No one ever wrote anything near to as-good-as-it-can-be on the first draft.

Since first drafts are always lousy, have students plan on giving themselves room to revise when they draft. Double (or even triple) space all draft writing. Even better, ***don't*** write the first two or three drafts. Record them orally and only write the story once the student has recorded a reasonably acceptable oral draft. (See TIP #6.)

Remember, writing is not the goal, the actual product. The story (or other narrative) is. Writing is only the chosen media to communicate the actual product. Don't ever allow the media to interfere with creation and development of the actual product!

TIP #3. DON'T STOP WRITING ON THE FIRST DRAFT TO CHECK SPELLING OR GRAMMAR

First drafts are all about passion (emotion and energy). Prewriting (before the first draft) is about planning. Postdrafting (evaluation, revision, and editing) is about precision. That wonderful first draft is the time for writers to *feel* the emotion of their story and to let their passions flow. Let your emotions out as you sling words at the page. Don't worry about the sentences, word choices, details, or spelling. Those are tasks for postdrafting. Worry about the energy, emotion, and passion of each scene.

Stopping to revise, to edit, even for a quick spell check always brings with it the unintended consequence of flattening the writing, making it dull and listless. If the fun, energy, and excitement aren't driven into the writing during that exuberant fling that we call drafting, it is extremely difficult to create them later.

If you aren't sure of the spelling, circle the word to check later and *keep writing*! If you aren't sure how to word the next sentence, skip it, leave several blank lines, and go on with what you can clearly see in your head. The idea of drafting is to let what you do know and what you can clearly see flow onto paper.

Certainly, no writer sits and drafts an entire novel, report, article, essay, or story in one sitting, in one great gush of writing. It is most common to break the whole into manageable chunks (scenes, sections, chapters, etc.) and to draft one, stop, and regroup before diving into the draft of the next chunk. It is also common to draft these chunks out of order. Start with the parts that are clearest and most vivid in your mind and draft those first. Draft each part only when you are ready, armed with vivid and detailed imagery and a strong sense of the flow and emotion of that part.

When you do, then, draft each part, don't stop to revise or rethink the writing. Focus on the characters, their emotions, and on the sensory details you would notice if you were really there—and write!

Later you can evaluate, revise, and edit to make the writing say exactly what you want it to say. It is so much easier for student writers, however, to separate these steps. Plan first, draft second, and do the grinding work of revision and editing later.

TIP #4. ON ASSESSMENT ESSAYS, *DON'T* ANSWER THE QUESTION

WHAT? Isn't the whole point to answer the question? No. It isn't. The point is to assess—to grade—your ability to write. They want to see you write, not provide a simple answer. Honestly, no grader will fact check your essay and mark you down for getting a date wrong. They won't mark you down if the experiences you describe in your writing don't measure up to the expectations of the grader. However, they will mark you way down if your description of those experiences doesn't measure up to the expectation of the grader. They care about your writing.

If students start by answering the topical question, they often become instantly stuck, not knowing where to go or what to do next.

If the essay prompt was, for example, *tell about a time you were scared*, a legitimate answer would be "Yesterday a car honked right behind me." That's an answer—an accurate and truthful answer. But it is not what they asked for. What they really asked is "Using 'tell about a time you were scared' as a general topic, show us how well you can write!"

There is no "right answer" to those writing essay questions, anyway. Think of the prompt as a springboard to launch your writing. Think first about how you'll take advantage of this springboard to make it as easy as possible for you to write a strong, effective essay. Treat the prompt as a seed that starts your planning process. Plan what you'll specifically write about, and how you'll write about it so that you can show off the best of your writing ability and your understanding of effective story structure.

TIP #5. EFFECTIVE NARRATIVES ARE WRITTEN AROUND THE EIGHT ESSENTIAL ELEMENTS

Here's the tip: develop the habit of planning *all* writing around the Eight Essential Elements. Two questions pop up: 1. Why? 2. What are they?

Here's the "why." The human brain is hardwired to make sense out of new information in specific story terms—the Eight Essential Elements. Extensive research and numerous studies have confirmed this statement. It's not that all readers **can** do it. It is that they automatically, without exception, **will** do it. If you develop the habit of planning for those same specific bits of information that the reader's mind requires, you will consistently deliver that key information to readers and they will be able to understand, make sense of, and become engaged by your writing.

So, what are those Eight Essential Elements? I have written several entire books on them. Here in briefest summary form:

1. **The Central Characters** who populate the key character positions in the story. *{Who am I writing about?}*

2. **The Character Traits** that make these characters interesting (memorable) to readers. *{What makes that character **interesting**?}*

3. **Goal**—what central characters want/need to do or get in this story. *{What do they **need or want to do or get** in this story?}*

4. **Motive**—why each of those goals is critically important to the character. *{Why is that goal so **important**?}*

5. **Problems & Conflicts** that block a character from reaching his or her goal. (The story's antagonist is the embodiment of the biggest of these conflicts.) *{What **problems and conflicts** keep the character from reaching his or her goal?}*

6. **Risk & Danger**—(the probability of failure and what happens if a character fails) created by the problems and conflicts for the main character. *{How do those problems and conflicts create **risk and danger** for the main character?}*

7. **Struggles**—what the character *does* (the action, the plot) to get past problems and conflicts, facing risk and danger, to get to their goal. *{What does the character **do** to get past problems ad reach his or her goal?}*

8. **The Details** (sensory, character, scenic, action) that create mental pictures and make the story seem vivid and real. *{What **details** will create the key pictures in readers' minds to make the story seem real?}*

Those simple informational elements form the core structure of all successful stories and other narratives. It is actually a simple habit to develop. It also makes the process of creating narrative material easier by breaking "create your story" into smaller and easily manageable chunks. The resulting narrative is far more consistently effective.

TIP #6. TALK THE FIRST THREE DRAFTS

Here are three well-researched and well-documented reasons to talk the initial drafts of any writing.

1. Student oral vocabulary is typically far greater than is their writing vocabulary.

2. Their willingness to include detail orally is far greater than their willingness to take the time to include that same detail in their writing.

3. Every time they say (describe) a scene, event, character, or place, they automatically build a more specific, detailed image of that thing in their minds. Then they will have more detail, clear and more specific detail, and more vivid detail in their minds when they finally do write. Say their story out loud, talk about the story, talk about the characters, sketch characters and scenes, doodle it, act it out. All of these add new mental detail. We *plan* stories, but we *write* details!

How are students to orally talk the initial drafts and not forget what they have said? Simple. Use a tape recorder (actually, any voice recording device from their smartphone, video recorder, down to an old-fashioned tape recorder). They can say it, listen to it, and mentally edit their story three times faster than they can write it once. They can also video record themselves talking their way through the first several drafts in order to capture the gestures and facial expressions that might suggest extra important detail to include when they write.

When they finally do write, they don't have to hold the story in their minds. It's on tape. Now they can focus on each sentence and on strong action verbs and on including the details.

Logistically simpler alternatives to managing how each student will record and listen to their stories exist that are almost as effective. A number of effective games (especially ones like *One-On-One-On-One-On-One*, *The Scene Game*, and *The Detail Game*—all described in detail in my book *Write Right!*) have been created specifically for this purpose.

TIP #7. THINK SMALL, NOT BIG, WHEN PLANNING

I find that students tend to think of grand and epic stories—the sort of thing skilled novelists need 500 pages in order to tell. Students can't seem to stay away from grand, sweeping epics, from stories that would be difficult to stuff into a 130-minute movie, from the BIG story idea. They want to write stories of saving the world (or of conquering it). They feel compelled to include life-and-death struggles that roam across whole continents as they confront and destroy ultimate evil in every story.

Don't do it. They will never be able to write those stories. As a result, they write condensed summary overview versions—sure death by boredom to the reader.

The solution: think small (in terms of space, time, topic {goal}, and characters). By "small," I really mean *tiny*. Don't plan a story about a noble superhero knight who must raise an army to invade the vast fortress of the evil sorcerer and restore peace and freedom to the land. No. Far better to write a story about that knight picking out just the right pair of boots to wear for that invasion—and to focus on that one decision and that one moment exclusively. There is still plenty of room to develop conflict and struggle and to bring out character personalities and relationships. In fact, it is much easier to develop the essential aspects of story in small-scale stories than in grand epics.

Don't write about a person's whole life, or about a whole year. Write about one day in their life—or better yet, just a part of one day, or just one hour of a day. That's manageable. They can hold that whole story in their heads and still have a bit of mental room for creating and holding the details. In fact, once the focus of their story shrinks to this miniature size, they will be both forced and free to focus on the internal and external details that mark successful and effective writing.

Scaling stories down to a small and manageable level will let students focus on the all-important character details, sensory details, character thought processes (use TFSS; see TIP #8), and to build each of the Eight Essential Elements. Effective writing is about the small, moment-to-moment details that build to that big picture they so eagerly lust after.

TIP #8. REMEMBER "THURSDAY, FRIDAY, SATURDAY, SUNDAY" TO BRING CHARACTERS TO LIFE

Students naturally (and most unfortunately) focus their writing on the action—on *what* each character does. Here's the problem: the action doesn't create excitement. It doesn't make readers understand a story. It (alone) doesn't engage readers. It (by itself) won't make readers care about the story characters. It's your story *characters* that readers need to care about, not their actions. That is, readers will only value and care about story actions and events to the extent that those events explain and illuminate characters and their struggles to reach important goals.

How does a student writer induce readers to become engaged by, entranced by, and personally involved with their story characters? Actually, it's easy—and, yes, even intermediate-grade writers can consistently do it.

How? Readers need to know how characters think, perceive, feel, and express themselves, as well as what they actually, physically, do. That's true for every scene and for every story event.

Here is a simple mnemonic to help students remember to provide that character-based information in each story scene that readers need in order to be fully engaged by those characters and those scenes. It's the last four days of the week (if you begin the week on Monday).

Thursday, Friday, Saturday, Sunday: T F S S. Think, Feel, Sense, Say. When writing each scene and each event, consider (and tell readers) what the principal characters are thinking and feeling; how they sense and perceive the scene around them; and what they say—all before you tell us what they *do* (the action).

No writer gives readers all of this information at and for every event. But every writer should picture each of these TFSS pieces for every event and decide what readers will need (or want) to know.

With a bit of practice and some gaming, TFSS can become both automatic and an immensely powerful asset for student writing.

TIP #9. BE PICKY SHOPPERS!

You head out to shop for new clothes. Do you settle for the first items you grab as you enter a store? No. You shop! You go to your favorite stores. But you're willing to check out new ones as well. You poke through all of the racks. You compare. You try it on and see if you can use it, if it fits, if you really like it, if this is the best buy. You check out four or five stores. You get picky. And that makes for smart, successful purchases.

Be just as picky when shopping online for research information. Don't mindlessly grab the first five websites that come up on your search. Be skeptical. Be critical—just as you are when you clothes shop. Make each source convince you to use it. How reliable is this source? Do the information and the writing make sense? Where did this source get the information it presents? Do I trust those sources? Does this information fit with what I already know? Will this info be useful to me?

You'll find that you develop your favorite sites—those that consistently deliver reliable information that meets your needs (just as you develop a list of favorite clothes stores). Still, for any given information search, be willing to check out other sources. But be as skeptical when you do as you would when you check out a previously unknown clothes shop.

If you later find a flaw (an error, a misstatement), return it, as you would a shirt with missing buttonholes, and move on to other sources of information.

There are almost countless sources of information available through the Internet. Most—but certainly not all—are reliable and factual. Remember, anyone (from four-year-olds on up) can post anything on the web and claim that it is true and factual. Your job is to be a picky consumer and only use the good ones.

Just as a blouse whose seam splits wide open on the first wearing ruins your whole outfit, using one error-filled source can ruin your whole paper.

TIP #10. STRONG OPENING SENTENCES COME LAST, NOT FIRST

Everyone wants to open with a great "grabber." Every writer wants to hook readers from the very first sentence. Two problems:

1. You can waste a whole lot of your available writing time searching for a great opening hook—and never find it—and never get your paper written.

2. You can't find the best *opening* for your story until you see exactly how your story *ends*!

Effective openings have three jobs.

1. Launch readers into the events of this story.

2. Hook the reader with some combination of character-based suspense and excitement.

3. Set up the ending, the resolution of the story.

What does this mean? Accept that you won't come up with a great opening on the first draft. If you happen to, that's great! But you are far better off assuming that you won't.

What do you do? Write the first draft starting where you think you'll begin. But don't even try to get the opening right at this point. Just start writing and get into the story (or essay, or report). Once you have finished that first draft, and once you have decided that you like the way you end your story, *then* go back and rewrite the beginning.

You'll find that it is suddenly much easier to think of, and to write, that wondrous opening hook you hoped for.

Here is one final reason not to be overly concerned with the wording of your opening hook during your first draft writing. Most of the time we start stories in the wrong place. However, you'll never notice that until after you have finished the entire first draft. Typically, we find that we can cut out the first few paragraphs—or scenes, or chapters—and be left with a much stronger "grabber" of an opening spot.

Openings are important. It is always worth spending time and effort to create the best opening you can. But the best time to do that is not when you first begin to write. It is after you have finished the whole story.

TIP #11. THREE QUESTIONS FOR BEFORE YOU WRITE ANY ESSAY

Many students struggle to write essays. (Essays differ from articles in that essays call for the writer to make personal assessments and comments and to inject personal opinion, whereas articles tend to rely on factual analysis and observation.) As a result, many students simply throw themselves at essay writing, blurting out their opinions without developing their case in a logical way and without providing the evidence that could sway the reader to agree with the writer's opinion.

One great way to avoid this essay calamity is to develop the habit of answering three questions before beginning to write. Yes, you must answer them all. This system reminds me of a team of lawyers carefully building their case for a jury trial. You have to tell the jury what to think. But you also have to tell them why they should think that, and then you have to back it up with some good evidence.

The three questions:

1. **What do I *think*?** (What do you believe and want the reader to remember, learn, or come to believe?)

2. **Why do I think that?** (What led you to draw that conclusion or to come to that position and belief?)

3. **Can I show any evidence?** (This is where facts, information, and observation come in.)

Now you're ready to write and to lay out your case to convince every reader to agree with you.

TIP #12. WRITE A DIARY FOR YOURSELF. WRITE EVERYTHING ELSE FOR THE READER

The readers' mental images are what count. Not yours. Many writers (even some experienced adults) think that their job is to get their thoughts and ideas down onto paper—to write what they want to say. WRONG!

That kind of thinking is fine if you're writing it for yourself—if you're writing a personal journal or diary. But if you expect any other person to read what you write, then you are writing for *them* and not for yourself.

Why the distinction? You already know exactly what you want to write. You already have detailed, vivid images of it in your mind. Therefore, *any* words you write will be fine for you because almost any wording will pop those perfect images back up into your conscious mind since they already exist in your memory.

But some other reader knows nothing about your topic. They hold no pictures of it in their minds. They will rely exclusively on your writing to build those images. You have to write for *them*.

I was in a 4th grade classroom working with students on writing details. One boy wrote, "The dog went in the house." I asked him to add more details about the house and about the dog so that we could all see them in our minds. He looked at me as if I were the stupidest adult on Earth and said, "I don't need to write any more. I can already see them. It's my house and my dog!"

Your job is to add in the details that will make the reader (who doesn't know anything about you or your story) see images as clear and vivid as the ones you already hold.

It's not enough for *you* to be able to see them, yourself, when you read what you wrote—although that is a crucially important first step. You have to write so that every reader sees it as well as you do!

TIP #13. THERE IS NO "RIGHT" OR "WRONG" IN WRITING

Students are eager to get the "right" answer and to be sure they didn't put down the "wrong" answer. However, when creating stories—or when writing in general—there is no "right" or "wrong." There is only "does it work?" or "doesn't it work?"

What do I mean? All that really matters in a written piece is: does this writing engage readers? Does it hold their attention? Does it create the vivid mental images that the writer intended? Does it convey the content (the story, the information) accurately into the mind and memory of the reader? That is what I mean by "does it work?"

There is no "one way" or "one particular wording" that accomplishes that lofty goal. There are ways to organize and present a story or essay that writers over the centuries have discovered work very well. They serve as excellent models of good writing. Still, that does not mean that those models are "right" and others are "wrong."

Rather than searching for a "right" way to write something, students will be better served to explore alternate ways to say the same thing and see which they like and which creates the most pleasing response from their readers.

CHAPTER 3

THE WORKOUTS: PRIMARY-GRADE WORKOUTS

Workout #1: Character Is...Because

Quick Summary & Purpose

** **Purpose:** • Understand the kinds of information authors use to make their characters interesting and memorable.

Summary: Every story you read or tell is an opportunity for your students to better understand that stories are character-based events and how authors convey character information to readers. If students learn this basic tenet of writing early during primary grades, it will hold them in good stead through all future years and all future writing activity.

Key Grades

All primary grades (including kindergarten)

Time Required

No specific time allotment. Do this as part of normal story review and analysis.

Introduction

Stories are about characters. It is characters that draw and hold readers' attention. It is characters through whose eyes readers see a story. It is characters to whom all actions happen and that give meaning and significance to story events and actions. If student writers develop the habit of finding ways to make their characters interesting (literally, "of interest"), they will consistently be called "good writers."

But there's the rub. Students are typically very poor at thinking a) of the kind of character trait information that would make their characters interesting, and then b) finding effective ways to deliver that information to readers.

Yet this habit can begin literally in kindergarten. Traits are specific pieces of information about any pertinent aspect of a character. We all (including very young children) draw conclusions about the characters around us by watching what they do and how they do it.

It's easy to turn that natural human mental activity into a story development game.

Directions

Create a "Character" chart or board. When you read stories (short stories, novels, or even series books), focus the follow-up discussion on the characters before discussing the plot and events.

From *Writing Workouts to Develop Common Core Writing Skills: Step-by-Step Exercises, Activities, and Tips for Student Success, Grades 2–6* by Kendall Haven. Santa Barbara, CA: Libraries Unlimited. Copyright © 2015.

Use this format:

" (Character)   is (trait) because (s)he   (specific example) ."

Let the class provide both various specific examples (direct evidence from events in the story's text) and their interpretation of what each action means about the character in question (a trait).

I recommend that you separate *traits* (characteristics of a character that remain true and constant throughout a story) from *emotions/feelings* that can change from time to time over the course of a story. However, the same analysis structure can be used for both.

This growing class list becomes a compilation of excellent examples for students to model and try in their own writing. However, I have found that the activity of having students consciously link concrete sensory descriptions in a story's text to their personal interpretation of a character (something they do automatically in real life) is even more valuable to their writing skill development.

Post-Activity Review & Discussion

This workout looks specifically at how authors convey critical character information to readers. By making that transference conscious in the minds of students, you arm them with the ability to create and describe interesting characters when they write and with a better ability to comprehend and dissect narratives.

Quick Summary & Purpose

** **Purpose:** • In a tightly controlled format, students will create and write a story. Learning comes through understanding the elements of the defined format they must use.

Summary: The goal of this workout is not to create a story. It is to learn the core elements of effective stories by having students create a story under the tight mandates of a prescribed format. That format will, in fact, create (rather than stifle) student energy and creativity. It will build enthusiasm for the story, and it will result in far more successful story creations—ones to show off to parents as well as administrators).

Key Grades

Perfect for 2nd grade. Excellent for 3rd grade. Okay for 1st.

Time Required

One session of 30 minutes; two of 45 minutes.

Introduction

I have never found a student that didn't quickly become excited by this story and by this process and form for creating his story. Even the most reluctant writers get quickly sucked into this story and this structured format.

One of the best writing habits children can develop is to not throw themselves at the story, but to develop a systematic approach to creating the key story elements before they begin to write. That is the idea of this workout. There are a few essential pieces of story information (the Eight Essential Elements) that form the core structure of effective stories. By isolating those individual elements—each onto its own pages in this book—students gain a good feel for the elements, what they look like, and what they contribute to the story.

Each student will create a six-page story. Specific information that represents one of the essential elements (and only that specific information) will appear on each page. The focus of this workout will be on both the process of creating story (create first; write second) and on the specific informational elements that create effective stories—both key teaching points for emerging writers.

Directions

Preparations

You have to make the books ahead of time—one per student. A bit of work, yes. But not overly onerous. Each book consists of eight 8.5 x 11-inch sheets (printer paper). These sheets include:

- Title page (with an "About the Author" section on the back)
- The six formatted pages of the actual story
- One notes page at the back where students can make their planning notes as they develop the story

It is best for you to make one master for each of the three types of pages (title page, book text pages, and notes pages) according to Figure 3.1 below. Then copy the pages for the actual

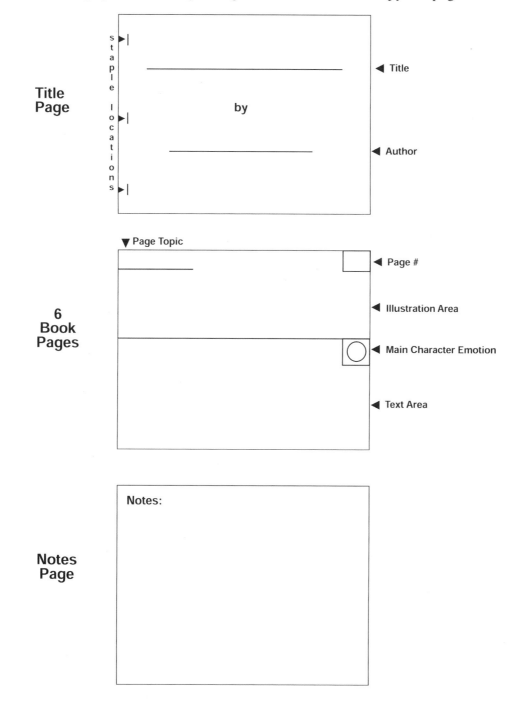

FIGURE 3.1 Page Format for the Six-Page Story

student books (one title page, six text pages, and one notes page per student book). That way you won't have to walk students through the process of placing the lines and boxes on each page.

The back side of each page is unused and remains unnumbered (except for the back of the title page that contains the "About the Author" section). Stack the eight pages for each book and staple 2-3 staples (as if binding a book) along the left edge (the 8 1/2-inch edge—not the 11-inch edge—so that the book will be a horizontal format book—wider than it is tall).

With that prep work completed, the workout can be performed in one extended session. However, most teachers prefer to break it into three shorter sessions over three sequential days.

First Session

Introduce the concept: each student will write a six-page book. But this book will have a special format. There is specific information that will go on each page. Each page will have only one kind of information on it.

You are going to hand out the books, talk about what will go on each page, and then—as a class—start the story!

Setting Up the Book

Have students start with the book closed so that they are looking at the title page. Have each student write his or her name (*the author's name*) on the lower line (below "by").

Open the book and look at the blank backside of the title page. Students will use this page for their "About the Author" section. However, don't write anything on that page now. You'll come back to it later.

Now look across at the first page of the book. Write the page number ("1") in the box in the upper-right corner of the page.

Ask students if they remember that only one specific kind of information goes on each page. Tell them that on this page (page 1) they will write information about the main character of the story. Write "Character Information" (or simply "Character") on the line in the top left of the page.

The back side of all pages in the book will not be used. They remain blank.

Turn to the next page. Write the page number ("2") in the top right box. Write the name of the kind of information ("Goal") they will write on this page along the top left side line.

Continue in the same way through the remaining pages of the book. Use the Story Element names for each page that are listed in the table below. Discuss what each informational element name means (See TIP #5), and emphasize that, on this page, they will write only this one kind of information about the story.

The purpose of this book organization is to isolate the key story elements so that students can think about and view them in isolation, remember what each element looks like, and better understand what each contributes to the story.

Page	Story Element	Description
0		Title and author
1	Main Character	Introduce the main character, initial setting, and list 2/3 key traits.
2	Goal	State main character's goal and why that goal is important to the character.
3	Problems	Describe the one big problem blocking character from goal and how that problem creates danger for the main character.
4&5	Struggles	What does the main character do to overcome problems and reach his or her goal?
6	Resolution	How does the story end? How does the main character feel at the end of the story?
7		Notes

Getting Started

Each student will develop and write his or her own version of the same story. However, each student will use these same two key pieces of story information:

1. Who the story will be about (the main character)

2. What that character needs to do or get in this story—and why that goal is important to the character (goal and motive)

Each student must now decide for their version of the story what (or **WHO**) is the one BIGGEST problem that blocks this common main character from reaching his goal. Identify this problem on the notes page, and describe what makes this problem dangerous for the main character.

Each student then creates two things (character traits) about the main character that he or she thinks makes this character different and interesting (what the character is afraid of; what she is good at; what she is bad at; what she is allergic to; things that make this character different from other characters; physical qualities that are unusual or unique; etc.). Write these two traits on the notes page.

With that work completed to launch the story, assign this homework question for students to ponder overnight: How will your character overcome the problem you created? Think about this story that you will write beginning tomorrow.

Second Session

Review the story structure: main character and goal. Allow several students to describe the problem they plan to use. Discuss what makes a good story problem (one that is dangerous and difficult to overcome). Talk about the story and possible actions to overcome the problems specific students have chosen. Allow students to add to their notes if they want to.

Review the book format and the story information that they will write on each page. ("On page one you will tell us who the main character is, where that character is, and describe the traits you invented. That's all that goes on page 1. On page two, you'll tell us about what the main character needs to do or get in this story and why it is so important to the character. And that is ALL that you write on that page. Etc.")

During this second session, however, no one writes anything. Today, students draw the picture that goes on each page. Beginning with page one (and knowing what information goes on that page—the main character and the initial setting for the story), use the space above the horizontal line (roughly the top 1/3rd of the page) to draw this picture. Don't write the story. Just draw the picture.

Then move on to page 2, where students will draw the picture that goes with telling readers about the main character's goal and motive. On to page 3 to draw the picture of the problem; then on to pages 4 and 5 to draw the pictures that go along with the character's struggles to overcome this problem. Finally, they draw the page 6 picture that depicts the ending of the story.

If time permits—and I strongly recommend that you create time for this step—pair students (or put them in small groups of three) and have them tell their story to other students as they turn the pages and show their pictures.

This ends the second session.

NOTE: Both telling and drawing are excellent ways to improve the vivid detail and specificity of each scene in the writer's mind. Create first; write second.

Third Session

It's time to write the story, page by page, one page at a time. However, before a student begins to write each new page of their book, he or she must decide how the main character feels at this moment in the story and draw the corresponding face in the small circle in the upper-right corner of the text box (lower 2/3rds of each page). The more consciously aware students are of the emotional state of their main characters, the more likely they are to incorporate this level of information into their writing.

Also remind students once again of the specific information that goes on each page and to be sure to stick with those informational limits.

Now they write the story text for page 1. As they write, they can glance back at their notes page for wording and ideas to build into their story text.

Then turn to the next page, draw the main character's emotional face, and write that page.

After they have finished the text for all six pages, they can turn to the back of the title page, write "About the Author" across the top, and write this section. Finally, they tear off and throw away the notes page and their book is finished and complete!

Post-Activity Review & Discussion

The most productive review activity for this workout is to review the informational elements associated with each page, what they look like, and how important they are as automatic parts of students' planning processes for any writing they do. These few, simple elements are actually the powerful core elements of all effective writing.

Quick Summary & Purpose

** **Purpose:** • A quick and fun way to improve student character development and description

Summary: Students routinely (almost automatically) place boring character description in their stories. ("He is weird." "She is funny." "He is good at sports.") It is the death of their writing and a total turnoff for readers. This is a fun, instant way to coax students away from those vague, general descriptions and toward the effective and interesting character descriptions they are all capable of producing.

Key Grades

Excellent for 2nd grade and up.

Time Required

15 minutes to demonstrate and discuss
2 to 5 minutes in small groups to use

Introduction

Every time I am in a classroom and force students to describe their character, they struggle to do it and to develop the character traits that make those characters interesting. However, when I talk one-on-one with students, they can *always* make their characters interesting. They have plenty of fascinating detailed information about those characters locked away in their minds. It simply never occurred to them that they must share this critical story information.

I used to be stumped as to why. Then I spent a week working in a small school in rural Maryland and trying to get 2nd graders to write stories. For the first three days, we never got past initially creating characters. I grew extremely frustrated and, on Wednesday of that week, exploded at one of the boys. He was no worse than any of the others. It seemed he was that final straw that broke this camel's back. As he tried to describe his character, it felt like the 10,000th time one of the students had said, "She is funny," or "He is good at sports," or "He is a liar," or, "She is weird."

And I exploded with, "Oh, yeah? Prove it!" The poor kid was terrified. Then, in a flash, it all made sense. He thought he *was* describing his character as he was supposed to do. I realized that his experience of stories had always been as the receiver of the story. Receivers of stories are tasked to synthesize the specific bits of detail the author provides in order to form general conclusions: He is funny; she is good at sports; he is a liar; etc.

When he shifted to being the author, he simply took his old job with him, never thinking that he should have left the synthesis job to *his* readers. It never occurred to him that it was now his job to provide those details for others.

If this sounds like your students, this is the game for you. Quick. Easy. And, oh, so productive.

Directions

The "game" revolves around a single line. Have one student describe a character he or she plans to write about. When the person states a general conclusion ("He is good at sports," "She is funny," etc.), interrupt and demand, "Oh, yeah? Prove it. Tell me what she *does*!!"

I have found that all students hold in their minds the specifics, the details, that support their general statements. After I demo this process with several students, I teach the whole class the key line:

"Oh, yeah? Prove it! Tell me what he/she DOES! I want specific examples!"

When I teach it to students, we add in lots of gestures and exaggerated body language. They love that part—and it makes it easy to learn and remember the line.

Now, turn them loose in small groups to use it on each other. Let them work one-on-one on their characters. Watch their character development—and their story development—skyrocket!

Post-Activity Review and Discussion

The best post-workout discussion for this workout is to read stories and then discuss exactly what information the author gave readers about the characters and how that information was delivered.

Have students imagine sitting with the author using this exercise. Can they imagine what the author would have said if they had used "the line" on this story author? Can they see how the author provided some specific examples to lead readers to their general conclusions?

Workout #4: Build a Snowman

Quick Summary & Purpose

** **Purpose:** • Students dramatically learn that their words hold a different meaning for the reader than they do for the writer.
- Students learn the power of effect of their specific details.
- Students see the power of vivid sensory images and detail.

Summary: In this workout, students will describe in step-by-step detail how to do something they all already know how to do: build a snowman. The seeming ease of the assignment makes it appealing to students. Yet the power of the workout comes when they realize how imprecise their directions were—specifically because they already know exactly how to build a snowman. It is a vivid and memorable demonstration of the Curse of Knowledge: once you know, you tend to write as if the reader knows as much as you do and, so, don't give readers what they need.

Key Grades

Excellent 2nd & 3rd grade; okay 1st.

Time Required

Three sessions of 30 minutes each.

Introduction

While this workout focuses on directions for how to build a snowman, you can substitute any other fun experientially based activity that all of your students feel they know exactly how to do. I created this workout as a slightly easier activity to describe than making a PB&J sandwich. (See Workout #13.) Use either (or both) with your class.

The general idea is to describe a seemingly simple action. However, through the three rounds of their writing these seemingly-simple directions, you will demonstrate for them virtually everything they will ever need for consistently effective writing (not necessarily glamorous or soaring writing, but consistently effective writing) by pointing out how imprecise their directions were.

Directions

Assignment

The starting assignment is simple: describe the process of building a snowman. It's okay if some children have never done it. They can imagine the whole thing. (They have all seen it on TV. You can shift to some other commonly-experienced activity as long as it is both simple and fun—emphasis there on the "fun" part.)

From *Writing Workouts to Develop Common Core Writing Skills: Step-by-Step Exercises, Activities, and Tips for Student Success, Grades 2–6* by Kendall Haven. Santa Barbara, CA: Libraries Unlimited. Copyright © 2015.

Step 1: The Basics

The Assignment

By the numbers, write detailed directions for making the best-ever snowman.

That's the assignment. If they ask for clarification, say that you want them to write down in exact sequential order each step for making what they think is the ideal (the best) snowman ever made. Yes, they can (even should) number the steps as they write them.

That should be sufficient. Have them double space when they write these directions.

Students must save all of their writing for this activity. They will write their directions three times. The most powerful teaching will come at the end when they compare the three versions.

Set a time limit for their writing. I usually use 20 minutes. However, feel free to vary that based on your knowledge of your class.

Invariably, someone will claim to not like making snowmen. For them, the best snowman is the one you make and then destroy. But they still have to write directions for making that snowman first. As the final direction, these writers will instruct readers to destroy all traces of the snowman and then go do something else that is more fun.

Evaluation & Post Discussion

Overnight, look *very literally* at what each student has written and try to identify the unstated assumptions each has made. Identify as many of these on each student's page as you can. Don't grade the papers at this point. Comment only on—but profusely on—the imprecision of their directions.

Many, for example will say to "make big snowballs" without describing how to roll and to control the growing balls or saying what the best size is for the snowballs to make an ideal snowman. Most forget to say that you have to go outside before you begin. Most write that you should put the snowballs on top of each other—without also telling you to make sure that they don't fall off. Many say to stick twigs or small branches into the snowman's sides for arms—without specifically instructing you to stick one "arm" into each side of the *middle* snowball . . . That sort of thing.

Be as picky as you dare, based on the writing competency level of your students.

Next day, you will need to bring to school three snowballs and a couple of twigs. (Styrofoam balls and stretched-out paperclips will do.)

Return the papers; give students a chance to look over all of your notes and marks; and then start a discussion with this live demonstration:

Find one of their papers that says to put the snowballs on top of each other and to stick the arms into the sides. Read those directions and then follow them literally. Place the balls and let one (or both) of the top ones fall off. Don't pick them back up. (The instructions didn't say to.) Jam both "arms" into the same side of the "head" snowball.

You get the idea of the demo. Do as many as you want. Literally and exactly follow a student's written directions to demonstrate the lack of precise and complete details. These demos are fun to watch and graphically point out the serious lackings in the level of detail students provided.

Now launch a discussion along these core themes:

1. The Curse of Knowledge. Each student already holds a detailed mental image of each step. *Any* words they write will pull that picture into their minds and *seem* to be totally adequate. Whatever they write will make perfect sense to them—because they already know! The "trick" to successful writing is figuring out what you have to write so that someone who doesn't already know will form the same mental images that you already hold.

2. What do readers really need? Why can't they see it as well as you? Discuss what information (in general) readers need in order to form vivid, interesting mental images. Have students try to identify (from their own reading experience) what pops rich and engrossing pictures into their minds while they read.

Step 2: Give Me Details or Give Me Reading Death!

The Assignment

It's time to rewrite their directions.

Rewrite your directions being clear and precise so that anyone will be able to follow your directions and successfully make a snowman.

Use the same time limit as before. No other directions or discussion should be needed.

Evaluation & Post Discussion

Again over night, read these version 2 directions to make sure that they have significantly increased the specificity of, and level of, detail in their directions. There is no need to comment back to each student on this version. In this version, they, typically, focus on physical, factual details. They often read as if the student were giving directions to a robot. However, in so doing, they typically overlook describing their sensory experience and reaction to the process and to their snowman. The writing is usually much more accurate. But it is not engaging, not compelling, and, well, typically boring.

Lead a short in-class discussion on what makes a narrative exciting and fun to read. It is not the action. It is the character and sensory detail that places vivid images in our minds and sets us up to be excited by the other elements in a story.

Step 3. The Sales Pitch

The Assignment

Time for the students to make one final rewrite of their directions. The goal of this rewrite is to move from precision to engaging and persuasive.

Rewrite your directions one more time. In this rewrite, convince me that <u>yours</u> *is the best set of directions for building the most gloriously wonderful snowman in the world. Convince me that I will adopt your directions as the only way I will ever again want to build a snowman.*

They write their directions a third time, focusing this time not on the factual directions—supposedly already there—but on the reader's sensory experience of both the process and the product.

Here are two cueing questions that I often read (or hand out) to help students think of strong, visceral description.

1. What does the snowman remind you of? What do you do with it once it's made? How much snow do you need to build a perfect snowman? Can you describe the perfect snow to make a snowman?

2. What does it feel like, sound like, and smell like while you are building your snowman? What does it sound like and feel like when you pile one snowball on top of another? How cold do your hands get? Does it make you laugh when you stick on its eyes and nose?

Post-Activity Review and Discussion

Both you and each student should compare the three versions. Which is more fun to read? Which engages you and holds your attention? Look at powerful, forceful words and images in version #3 compared to the bland and uninteresting words in version #1. Now revisit the discussion on what builds a vivid image. What makes you want to read something? What holds your attention?

While you can grade either the quality of each student's version #3 writing or (I think preferably) the improvement from version #1 to version #3, I think this is best kept as an ungraded—but powerful—demonstration of students' natural writing style (version #1) and the impact of focused revision and editing (version #3).

Workout #5: Spelling Stories

Quick Summary & Purpose

** **Purpose:** • This workout simultaneously develops both mastery of this week's spelling list and effective story form and structure.

Summary: By 2nd grade, students get weekly spelling and vocabulary lists. They are a drudge. They are a downer. This is a way to make those lists of words both fun and creative and also serve double duty: it's far easier to learn the words *in story context* and, at the same time, develop a better sense of effective story structure.

Key Grades

2nd and up.

Time Required

In class: none to write; 20 minutes to share.

Introduction

You assign spelling words every week. Learning those lists is always hard. Why? Research confirms that we learn best when we have context and relevance for the new information. By definition:

Context: How this new information (word) fits in with what I already know.

Relevance: How this new word is relevant to me (what it means to *me*).

Stories create both relevance and context for both new concepts and new vocabulary. Use story form and structure to help cement new vocabulary into students' minds. It is the mandate to create a decent story (use the Eight Essential Elements—see TIP #5) that gives this game real power

Directions

Spelling lists are boring. Stories are fun. Combine the two and the result serves triple duty:

1.   It's more fun to learn the spelling words this way.

2.   You improve learning because words are learned *in story context* instead of on an abstract list.

3.   Students inadvertently work on mastering effective story structure.

From *Writing Workouts to Develop Common Core Writing Skills: Step-by-Step Exercises, Activities, and Tips for Student Success, Grades 2–6* by Kendall Haven.

36   Santa Barbara, CA: Libraries Unlimited. Copyright © 2015.

Instead of sending students home to memorize weekly spelling lists, tell them to create a story using every one of the spelling words. The story has to make sense and has to use each and every one of the spelling words. Students should underline each spelling word as they fit it into their story.

Shorter stories are better. Tell students to see how short they can make the story and still get all spelling words in! Be creative!

Let selected students read their stories to the class. The class has three assigned tasks during this reading:

1. Decide if the reader does, in fact, use all of the assigned vocabulary.

2. Decide if they used each vocabulary word correctly.

3. Decide if they incorporated the key story elements in their story.

Focus the post-reading discussion on the story (not the vocabulary words). Work on the Eight Essential Elements of effective stories (character and the traits that make them interesting; goal and the motives that make that goal important; conflicts and problems that block the character and the risk and danger they create; how the character struggles to reach his or her goal; the details that create mental images for readers). (See TIP #5)

As an option, allow students to build "chapter books" with subsequent week's lists—adding one new chapter each week.

Post-Activity Review and Discussion

You require that students learn their vocabulary words. This game will improve their vocabulary learning and also give you repeated opportunities to demonstrate and discuss effective story structure and the elements that create that effective structure.

CHAPTER 4

WORKOUTS PERFECT FOR BOTH PRIMARY AND INTERMEDIATE GRADES

Workout #6: The BIG Three

Quick Summary & Purpose

** **Purpose:** • Demonstrate the power of beginning a story with core character information.

Summary: If students begin their stories by creating core character information, they greatly increase the probability that they will produce a successful story. However, this isn't a "natural" place for students to start. They want to start by creating plot, the surest way to undermine their own story. This exercise helps them establish a new and better habit.

Key Grades

Excellent for all elementary grades 1 through 6. Okay for kindergarten

Time Required

Part I: 15 to 20 minutes. Regular repetition is best.
Part 2: 15 to 30 minutes

Introduction

Students typically want to start their story creation by creating a plot line—the action, what happens. It is the surest way to create boring stories. It is a formula for reader boredom. It is important to shift their most basic thinking away from plot and _to characters_. This workout represents a big step along that pathway.

Directions

Bring three students to the front of the class and announce that they are going to create a story for the class.

Each student will create one of the three core character elements: identify the main character, define that character's goal, and create obstacles and problems. However, the specific wording you use in soliciting these bits of information is important.

The goal of this exercise is to demonstrate that these three essential character elements always launch and define a story. Reinforce that concept regularly.

The wording I have found that works the best is as follows.

To the first student: "The other two students are going to make up a story. All you have to do is make up that first, most important, bit of information they need, which is . . ." Here I pause to let student and class mull over what information should come first. "Which is . . . the character.

From _Writing Workouts to Develop Common Core Writing Skills: Step-by-Step Exercises, Activities, and Tips for Student Success, Grades 2–6_ by Kendall Haven. Santa Barbara, CA: Libraries Unlimited. Copyright © 2015.

Every story needs to start with *who* the story is going to be about. This character you're going to make up can be, but doesn't have to be, a human being. It does have to be a fictional, never before made up, character. It could be an animal—a dog, a frog, an elephant, a snake, a snail, or a mosquito. It could be a bush or a tree. It doesn't even have to be alive. It could be a cloud, a chair, or your shoelace. You can have them make up a story about anything. But it does have to be a brand-new fictional character. What do you want them to make up a story about?"

Let student #1 now create a character's first impression: the species identity, name, age, and just enough physical information so everyone envisions the same character. You can veto any character you don't like. I always veto aliens because it takes too much background information for everyone to understand the species, their world, and their basic life patterns and needs. Also veto all previously created fictional characters and any attempt to use real people (or model a fictional character after a real person—most often a classmate).

You repeat and summarize whatever they pick. "Once there was a young, floppy-eared rabbit named Seymore."

To the second student: "Now the second bit of essential character information: *In this story*, what did Seymore need to either do or get? It doesn't have to be anything that would make sense for a rabbit to want to do or get. He could *want* to do *anything*. What do you want Seymore to **need**—to be after—in this story?"

Your wording here is important. If you ask for the character's goal (what you really want), you'll get nothing but blank stares. Ask for what the character needs to either do or get and you'll get great answers.

Again summarize the created information thus far. "Once, there was an old, floppy-eared rabbit named Seymore who wanted to eat some chocolate chip ice cream. He was tired of carrots and lettuce. He was tired of always going to the salad bar. He wanted dessert. He wanted some ice cream!"

To the third student: "Now the third bit of essential character information. Why hasn't Seymore gotten any ice cream? What's keeping Seymore from getting his ice cream? Something must, or he'd already have it. So what's keeping Seymore from getting any ice cream?"

You are asking for obstacles, either problems or conflicts. The wording shown above will spark their creation. Asking directly for a problem or obstacle typically won't.

Allow the student to make up three or four potential obstacles. Stop the student anytime he or she drifts into a plotting sequence (a series of events that could happen in the story). You want only the potential obstacles, not how they will fit into the story.

Again summarize for the class. "Once there was an old, floppy-eared rabbit named Seymore who wanted to eat some chocolate chip ice cream. He was tired of carrots and lettuce. He wanted dessert. He wanted some ice cream! BUT Seymore had no money to buy ice cream.

And his mother said he couldn't have any because it was bad for him and would rot his teeth. Besides, the ice cream store owner hated rabbits and would shoot any rabbit that came near his store. But Seymore *really* wanted some ice cream."

If you find (as most often happens) that this student has created only problems confronting the character (e.g., he has no money, he doesn't know where the ice cream store is, etc.), ask, "**Who** doesn't want Seymore to get his ice cream?" This will always shift their focus from problems to conflicts.

Now turn to the class and ask, "How is this story going to end? What's the last thing that will happen at the end of this story?"

They will answer, "It ends when Seymore gets some ice cream." Most likely, they will try to include the plotting sequence that explains *how* Seymore will get his ice cream. Cut such discussion short. You want only what happens at the very end.

Now say, "Getting ice cream is one of two possible endings for this story. Does anyone know the other?" The other, of course, is that Seymore *never* gets any ice cream. It usually takes a while for students to come up with this option. If any suggest that the story ends when Seymore dies (and 4th, 5th, and 6th grade boys surely will), ask if, after he dies, Seymore still wants some ice cream. That will fit their answer back into one of the two plausible endings for the story.

The main character's goal defines the story's end and creates structure for the story. Stories end when the main character's primary goal is resolved—one way or the other.

Open up the discussion for other possible obstacles and problems, both internal and external. Stop anyone who begins to present a plotting scenario. They should only be allowed to suggest other obstacles that could keep the character from reaching his goal.

As a class, discuss which obstacles will make for a better story. Consistently it will be those obstacles that create the greatest risk and danger for the character. Risk and danger create the excitement and tension every story needs to propel a reader through to a powerful and satisfying climax.

Ask if any students think they know how the story will go. Many will say yes. Don't allow them to launch into their version of the story. Rather, ask them *why* they think they know how the story goes. The discussion will lead back to the chosen obstacles.

Obstacles create plot.

Part 2: The Big 3 *Plus*

Back to student #2. Ask, "Why does Seymore want ice cream?" You are now searching for motives to support the goal. Let the whole class participate. Note for the class that any suggested motives that make the goal more critically imperative create *suspense* and greatly increase interest in the story.

Finally, if time permits, turn back to student #1 and say, "Seymore (our character) isn't very interesting to me yet. I don't know enough about him to care one way or the other. Tell me something interesting about Seymore."

This launches the class into an exploration of character traits. I usually take control of this discussion and write categories of character information on the board one at a time and let students create four or five traits for each. Those that I typically present (in this order) are: fears, flaws and frailties (I start with allergies and then go to physical imperfections), things the character is good at (including academic subjects); things he is bad at (can't do well), physical description, things he's done that he is proud of, things he's done that he is ashamed of, passions and loves, things he hates, etc. You may use whatever categories you want. See the "Character Trait" section in *Get It Write* for a listing of potential categories.

You will find that the class goes wild for this activity. Ideas fly. Everyone thinks of more outrageous answers than the next person. Your jobs are:

1. Make sure that all suggestions are plausible and fit the category you are working on. I demand that students explain any answer that doesn't make good sense to me. (If, for example a student says that the character is allergic to air, I demand to know why he hasn't already taken care of this allergy since he has always been exposed to air. I also demand specifics on what the effect of the allergy would be.)

2. Play scribe and ringmaster. Keep order and keep the lists moving.

3. Point out to the class how much fun it is to create character traits. Most of them think of this task as boring drudgery. But no! This is where authors pump fun, energy, and delight into their stories.

During the whole exercise your job is to keep the story moving and to prevent students from interjecting plot. No plot is mentioned or discussed during this exercise. However, once these basic character elements have been created, every student intuitively "knows" what has to happen in the story.

Post-Activity Review and Discussion

Creating character always creates an effective story. Creating a plot (a series of actions) does not. One of the most valuable writing habits you can instill in your students is to always start with character, goal, motive, and interesting character traits; then expand to problems and conflicts; and only then to the action and plot.

Workout #7: Fred du Frog

Quick Summary & Purpose

** **Purpose:** • Clearly and forcefully demonstrate the Eight Essential Elements

Summary: This is the best and the most powerful single activity I have ever created. It clearly, and in a fun way, demonstrates the Eight Essential Elements of effective stories. In an interactive class activity, you will get them to identify each element as you build a story.

Key Grades

Excellent for 2nd and up.

Time Required

Part 1: 45 to 60 minutes
Part 2: 45 to 60 minutes
Part 3: 30 minutes

Introduction

It is always best to learn the Eight Essential Elements of stories by seeing them in action to build a fun story. That is the concept of this workout.

I have used this game format workout many hundreds of times. It always works. It is always fun. It always gets the entire class excited. I give it to you with the wording I use that has proven itself to be most effective. You may either read your part as if it were a script or improvise it into your own words. Most importantly, remember to have fun with Fred. Play with the situations and with student suggestions.

As you glance at these directions, they may appear to be long and arduous. Don't be intimidated. I have made the directions both explicit and detailed. The activity itself flows smoothly, easily, and quickly in actual practice. And the results are ALWAYS worth the effort!

Finally, I encourage you to play with this developing story. Feel free to add small asides. Exaggerate scenes and your descriptions of events. Make it fun for you and for your students and they will be both riveted and they will learn!

Directions

Part I: The Eight Essential Elements

This is the core part of this workout, the one during which you demonstrate and build seven of the Eight Essential Elements. The wording I use (your lines) are indented and italicized and introduced with "Teacher":

Vertically, along the left-hand margin of the board write the numbers 1 through 8. As you develop each of the Eight Essential Elements, you will write that element's name on this list next to the appropriate number.

> **Teacher:** *We are going to build a story. While we do, I want to show you the eight bits of information the minds of your story readers need in order to understand and to like your stories.*
>
> *We need to start by starting our story.* (You can pretend to ponder for a moment as if just creating this idea.) *This will do. Once, there was a frog . . . a frog named Fred. Fred du Frog. Now, Fred du Frog was a big frog . . . a B-I-G frog. And this day Fred was sitting on a wide lily pad in the mud.*
>
> (Pause as if you have just gotten a new idea.) *Let's put this mud along the shore of a lake. A nice lake, a medium-sized lake. Thick woods come right down to the shore of the lake all around it—except on this side where there's a thick strip of mud, and except for straight across the lake where there is a small meadow.*
>
> *In the mud sits Fred du Frog on his lily pad. In fact, he covered up the whole lily pad because he was a B-I-G frog.*
>
> *Sitting around him in the mud were three itty-bitty little frogs. Three itty-bitty frogs and Big Fred—That's what he liked to call himself—Big Fred. Those three itty-bitty frogs called him Big Fred. Fred's friends, the birds, up in the trees at the lake, they called him Big Fred.*
>
> *Yup, Big Fred sittin' on his lily pad with those three little frogs sittin' in the mud around him. . . . The End.*

Now ask if that is a complete and satisfying story. (Students will say "No!")

> **Teacher:** *Before we look at what's still missing and what we need to add, let's look at what we **do** already have in the story.*

There are only three essential story elements that are present. There is no action or plot (Nothing has happened. We just have four frogs sitting in the mud.)

As soon as anyone mentions "details," acknowledge that student and write "Details" next to #8 in your vertical list of elements. Review the details about the lake and the frogs that are in the segment you have already read. Story details create the mental images (pictures) that readers depend on. More details create more vivid and expansive mental pictures.

As soon as someone mentions characters, enthusiastically acknowledge that student and write "characters" as the #1 element. Tell them that we also have some information about the story characters. We call these "character traits." Write "Traits" as Element #2.

Teacher: *Who do you think will be the main character of this story?*

Let them answer. (Students will say "Fred du Frog.") Ask them why they think that. Let them mull over that question and pose answers. Ask if they think that Fred is an interesting character. (Responses are typically mixed.) That, however, sets up this next important question. Say that the job of the traits is to make the character interesting to readers. Write "(interesting)" next to Traits on the board.

Teacher: *We only have one bit of information in this story that helps make Fred even a little bit interesting. What is it? I am now looking for the $2 million word.*

Students will first want to know if they really get the two million. I respond that my job is just to ask the questions. Someone else is supposed to come out from backstage and hand out the cash if anyone gets it right. Of course, this answer is worth two million to every writer whether or not they actually get the cash.

The $2 million word is "different." Making a character different (in any way) from those around him makes the character be of interest to the readers. It makes it possible for readers to visualize and hold onto that character.

Have students struggle to come up with the word. About half the time in 5th and 6th grades, someone will come up with the idea that having Fred be a big frog while all the other frogs are itty-bitty makes him different, and that makes him interesting. That rarely comes without prompting in lower grades.

When they need a hint, ask them how many frogs are in the story. Someone will quickly and correctly answer "4." Ask that student to describe three of the frogs. He or she will say that three of the frogs are small. Then ask the student to describe Fred. The student will say that Fred is a big frog.

Teacher: (This wording is important.) ***And that makes Fred** . . . .?*

By this time, half the class will be rattling their hands in the air wanting to shout out the answer. Many of their answers will be wrong ("It makes him the daddy" or the boss or the king). If anyone says "It makes him interesting," you respond by saying, "Yes, because it makes him . . . . ?"

Eventually, someone will say "different." Have that student stand for a bow and a round of applause as you write "Different" on the board next to "Interesting." I usually draw an arrow from "different" back to "interesting," and from "interesting" back to "traits."

Tell them that now we can go on with the story. Ask the class if the story is exciting so far. They will answer "No!"

Teacher: *Before we go any further, I want to make sure that this is going to be an **exciting** story. What creates excitement in a story?*

If anyone says "Danger," either pretend not to hear them or answer "Good, we'll try that and see if it works. Is there anything else that can create excitement in a story?"

You want someone to say "action." Even if they don't all say it, my research shows that most elementary and middle school-aged children believe that action creates excitement. This is a great opportunity to demonstrate how actions do not create excitement and risk and danger do.

After someone dutifully suggests action, do this for a demo.

Teacher: *Let's see if action makes the story exciting. (Say this part in a deep, slow, dramatic, intense voice.) Fred stood up from his lily pad. He walked the length of the mud along the shore of the lake until he came to a large . . . raspberry bush. Fred climbed up to the top of the raspberry bush. He looked around the lake. He hopped back into the mud. He walked back to his lily pad. And Fred du Frog— Big Fred—sat . . . back . . . down!*

Ask if that was exciting. They will answer "No." However, it was pure action. Fred stood, walked, climbed, looked, hopped, walked, and sat. All actions. If action could make a story exciting, those should have because they were pure action.

Students will protest that those were boring actions. I often let students suggest "better" actions because I know that I can take any suggestion they offer and, if I say only the action part, I can easily make every suggestion sound trivial, silly, and boring. You can certainly do that if you want to.

At some point, stop the discussion and tell them that the reason the action was boring is because:

Teacher: *Action, alone, is **always** boring to readers. Action cannot, will not, and never has created excitement. It's not supposed to. That's not it's job in a story. There is this "OTHER THING" we need to create first. Once we create that "OTHER THING," then any action we put in the story will <u>seem</u> to be exciting because we put that "OTHER THING" in first.*

That *"OTHER THING,"* of course, is danger (technically, risk and danger), the likelihood that something will go wrong and what happens to the character when it does.

Best if you create that core danger in order to keep control of the story.

Teacher: *See if this makes our story exciting. Do you know why Fred was sitting in the mud instead of swimming in the cool, sweet waters of the lake? Because in the lake there lived a crocodile! A 3-ton, 24-foot long crocodile with long rows of huge,* *gleaming, jagged, razor-sharp teeth. That crocodile was a frog-eating crocodile who had already eaten most of the frogs at the lake.*

Now you might think that all of the frogs who were left—who hadn't been eaten by the ferocious crocodile—would just leave the lake and go live by a stream in the woods. But they couldn't. Because in the woods there were . . . bears. Frog-eating bears!

And now there were only four frogs left alive at the lake—Big Fred sitting on his lily pad and those three itty-bitty frogs sitting around him in the mud. Every other frog had already been eaten—either by the crocodile in the lake or by the bears in the woods!

Ask if this is more exciting. They will answer "Yes." Point out that nothing has yet happened in our story. No action yet. You simply told them the way things are.

You are now working toward two additional elements (#5: Problems and Conflicts, and #6: Risk and Danger). Those two elements go together—just as Character (Element #1) and Character Traits (Element #2) go hand in hand, as do Goal (Element #3) and Motive (Element #4), which we will get to in a bit.

Ask them what you created for the story that wasn't there before.

Skip over answers like "two new characters" and "excitement." You want someone to say that you created a PROBLEM. (Technically, the two problems you created are CONFLICTS.). If they need a hint, write a "P" on the board next to the #5 in the list of Elements, and tell them the word you need starts with a "P."

Once you have gotten someone to say "problem," write "Problems and Conflicts" on the board as the fifth element. Then ask this:

Teacher: *What is the difference between having Fred stub his toe, or forgetting how to spell frog, and a vicious frog-eating crocodile in the lake? They are all problems. What makes the crocodile exciting and the other two not? What does a frog-eating crocodile create for Fred that forgetting how to spell "f-r-o-g" does not?*

Soon enough, someone will either say "danger" or one of its synonyms. Write "Risk and Danger" on the board as the sixth element. Problems and conflicts block characters and create risk and danger. Risk and danger create story excitement.

Tell them it's time to get back to the story. Start with a situational recap

Teacher: *Okay. Here's what we have. Fred and the three little frogs are sitting in the mud. Crocodile is swimming back and forth across the lake. ("I want to eat a frog . . . I want to eat a frog.") Bears are prowling through the woods. ("We want to eat some frogs . . . We want to eat some frogs.") So Big Fred and those three* *itty-bitty frogs sat happily in the mud, safely away from the crocodile in the lake and safely away from the bears in the woods for the rest of their lives. The End.*

Students will roar with outrage and reject that ending. However, that exact ending is important because it sets up this search for the three missing elements —**#3: Goal** (What the character needs or wants to do or get in this story), **#4: Motive** (Why that goal is important to the character), and **#7: Struggles** (What the character does to overcome problems and conflicts, facing risk and danger to reach an important goal).

First you must establish the fact that Fred is safe while he sits in the mud. Students will insist that either the croc or the bears will come after Fred in the mud. Here is your response:

Teacher: *No. The crocodile cannot get into the mud. Remember, he is 24 feet long and weighs 3 tons. He's too heavy. The mud is soft and squishy. If he stepped onto the mud, he'd sink in and die. He knows that and, so, never touches the mud.*

And everyone knows that frog-eating bears hate to get their paws muddy. So the bears never touch the mud.

They will complain that the story is boring. You agree and tell them that they have to fix it. I typically say:

Teacher: *The story isn't boring for Fred. He gets to live. It's only boring for us readers. You are the writers. You fix it. Something is still missing in this story. What is it? I am now looking for the $5 million word—the only way to fix this story and make it be as exciting as you want it to be. What's missing? Fix it!*

Let several students offer their plans to fix the story. Typically, the first offerings will constitute actions ("Fred attacks the crocodile" or "Fred goes on an adventure in the woods"). Each time a student suggests some dangerous action they want Fred to undertake, respond by asking:

Teacher: *Why would Fred do that? He is perfectly safe where he is. Every frog that has set foot in the woods has died. Every frog that has dabbled a froggy toe into the lake is dead. So, why would Fred do that?*

Notice that asking a "why" question always probes for goal and motive (what the character is after and why he or she needs it).

I find that most students are unable to answer that question in order to justify the action they propose for Fred. Look for someone to say either that Fred "wants" something or that he "needs" something (usually it will be food). When a student (even inadvertently) uses one of those two magic words, say, *"You are now Student #1. Hold that thought."* But do not yet tell the student that she has used one of the magic story-fixing words or what the word was that she used.

Move on and collect several more ideas on how to fix the story. Designate the 2nd student to use one of those two magic words as student #2. Then say:

Teacher: *Student #1 and student #2 each used an alternate version of the $5 million word. Before I open it up for anyone to guess the word, I will give them a turn to remember the magic word they used.*

Turn to Student #1.

Teacher: *Say your idea again. When you first said it, you used an alternate version of the $5 million word.*

Let the student repeat his basic idea. Tell the student if, this time, he did or did not again use the $5 million word. Then give him one chance to identify the magic word that he actually said. Just that **one word**. If he does, he wins. Most often, he won't. Turn to student #2 and repeat the offer.

If student #2 also fails, open it up to the whole class. If they need a hint, give them the first letter of the word student #1 & #2 actually used (either n for "need" or w for "want").

They'll get it with that clue. Write "Goal" next to Element #3 on the board, and explain that a character's goal is what **a character either needs or wants to do or get in this story**. Add want and need in parentheses next to "Goal."

Teacher: *If Fred doesn't **need** anything, then there is no reason for him to **do** anything! He won't face dangerous crocodile and bears unless there is some good reason for him to do it. He must need something.*

Let's use food as the thing Fred needs in this story. But he could need to do or get anything.

Let a variety of other students offer other things that Fred might want or need. Point out to them that changing goal changes what the story will be about. Stories are about a character's struggles to reach a goal. Goal defines story. Without a goal, the story is pointless and will never be exciting.

Ask students **why** Fred needs food. Tell them that asking why a character needs a goal leads to identifying MOTIVE. Write **Motive** next to #4 on the board. Motive explains why a goal is important to a character. The more important a goal is, the more suspenseful and exciting the story is. Say:

Teacher: *I want to make "getting food" really important to Fred. I want us to create a great motive for this goal. Why does Fred need food?*

As they offer reasons, push them to make each one more extreme. Ultimately you will all agree that they need food because without it they will starve. Then push the class to shorten the amount of time before the frogs all starve. You want to get to a point where everyone agrees that, if the frogs don't get food within a few hours (by lunchtime), they will all starve. That's motive!

Now go back to the story.

Teacher: *Let's review where we are. Big Fred and those three itty-bitty frogs are sitting in the mud. The crocodile is swimming in the lake. Bears are prowling in the woods. And let's put all the frog food across the lake in that small meadow . . . at a French Fly stand. If they don't get to that food by lunchtime they'll all starve.*

Now, here's what happens next. Fred's friends, the birds, flew across the lake, got the food, and brought it back. The frogs ate and lived happily ever after. The End.

Once again, your students will be outraged and totally reject that version. Ask them what's wrong with your version. You solved the problem and got Fred to his goal (food), didn't you? Reluctantly, they will agree. Yet, still they will grumble because the story was boring.

Teacher: *Would you be happier if I had the crocodile trap Fred and almost eat him? Would you be happier if I had the bears surround Fred and tie him onto a long stick to be barbecued over a campfire squished between two marshmallows?*

They will roar with approval. Point out that they don't want you to make it easier on Fred. They want—actually they require—that you make Fred struggle. The more he struggles, the better readers like it.

Write Struggle next to Element #7 on the board.

You now have identified all of the Eight Essential Elements. Before you move on to Part 2, offer this quick demonstration of what one scene might look like if Fred has to struggle. How do we present a character's struggles and make them exciting? With effective details (Elements #7 & 8 in action).

Teacher: *One of the little frogs said, "Ummmmm. 'Scuse me, Fred. But, ummm, if we don't get some food before lunchtime, we're all going to starve."*

Fred said (use a deep, gravelly voice), "Wellllll, I know we will. I've been thinking 'bout that."

"But, ummmmm, Big Fred All the frog food is waaay across the lake. And if you try to swim across the lake to get it, the crocodile is going to eat you."

"Wellll, I know he will. I've been thinking 'bout that."

"And, ummmmmm, Big Fred, if you try to walk around the lake, you have to go through the woods. Then the bears are going to eat you."

"I know they will. I've been thinking 'bout that, too."

Then Fred's face lit up. He said, "Boys, I got a plan. I've been thinking 'bout it.

The birds are my friends. They can carry me across the lake to get the food."

A dozen birds flapped down to the mud. Fred explained the plan. The birds agreed. Twelve birds picked up Big Fred, holding him in their little bird beaks, flapping their little bird wings, lifting Big Fred up higher and higher over the lake.

At that same moment, the crocodile glided hungrily across the lake, his stomach growling, his massive jaws gnashing and thrashing at the water, both of his eyes locked straight up onto Fred. "Lunchtime," grinned the crocodile to himself.

Now the birds are holding on with their little bird beaks, flapping their little bird wings as hard as they can, gasping and panting for breath as their little bird hearts pounded in their tiny bird ribcages, carrying Big Fred higher across the lake.

Pause here and ask students what they think is going to happen. They will answer that the birds are going to drop Fred. Ask them why they think that. They will say that they'll drop Fred because he is too heavy.

That answer sets up your final point of Part 1.

Teacher: *See what you did? As soon as I started this event, this action, you searched back through everything you knew about the character (Big Fred) for something you could use to get him into BIG TROUBLE. The only thing (the only character trait) you know so far is that he is a "big frog." The story comes alive and becomes exciting when a character gets in BIG TROUBLE.*

Can you imagine how easy it would be to get Fred into trouble if, instead of one thing, we knew 50 traits for Fred . . . or 100?! And that is exactly what we need to do next—invent more fun traits for Fred. Then we can decide what is going to happen in the story.

This completes Part 1. You have identified all Eight Essential Elements. You have created the basic structure of a most successful story. In Part 2, you and your students will take the next critical steps in fleshing out this framework into a workable story.

Part 2. Building Character & Story

Summary

Part 2 extends the story of Fred du Frog from basic framework into a developed story outline. Specifically, this part focuses on character development (that aspect of story development students most consistently overlook and underdevelop) and, then, on character-based plotting structure (rather than on action- or event-based plotting structure).

Set Up

You'll need lots of board space to write on for Part 2. Use the left-hand side for a vertical list of the Eight Essential Elements (as you developed them during Part 1). Use the middle section of the board for development of character trait information. Use the right-hand portion for the class's development of plotting ideas.

Review

Quickly review the Eight Essential Elements and the function and purpose of each. For more information on these elements I refer you to either *Story Smart: Using the Science of Story to Persuade, Inspire, Influence, and Teach* or to *Get It Write!* (two of my other Libraries Unlimited books).

Also review what the class has created for each element as part of the Fred du Frog story so that they are familiar with the step up of the story.

Plotting Plans

Start Part 2 work with words to this effect.

> **Teacher:** *Big Fred has only a few hours to get past the crocodile or to get past the bears, get safely across the lake to the food, and bring it back to the three itty-bitty frogs. How is Fred going to get that food?*

Let students suggest possible strategies (plans) for Big Fred to use. At this time, you **DO NOT** want the whole event, the action. You ***don't*** want to know what happens. You only want them to identify Fred's plan—his scheme, his strategy—before he sets out from his lily pad to get the food.

Critically consider each suggestion.

- If a suggestion requires the crocodile or the bears to cooperate (that is, requires that one of these antagonists perform specific actions), reject it. Those characters have no motive for cooperating with Fred's scheme. In fact, they are highly motivated to make sure Fred's plan fails! That's how they get their lunch.

- If it doesn't make sense or isn't clear to you, have the student explain what Fred's plan is. Don't let him drift into a description of the ensuing actions. Not yet. If he can't articulate a clear, simple plan, reject it.

- If the plan calls for someone else (the birds, for example) to do the work and get the food, reject it. Fred is our main character. Readers will want to watch him be the one to struggle to reach his goal.

- If a suggestion requires Fred to suddenly acquire superpowers or advanced weaponry, also reject those. Tell students:

Teacher: *Remember, story excitement comes from characters facing risk and danger. If Fred has superior powers, there won't be any real danger, and the story will be hard to write and boring for readers. Better to give superpower to the crocodile to increase the risk and danger Fred must face.*

List all plausible ideas in a word or two in a column along the board's right side. Typical example plans often include: build a boat, the birds carry him, create a decoy to fool the crocodile, get a disguise, get a bear costume and pretend to be a bear, build a kite and fly, etc.

If the class isn't creating sufficiently fun ideas, suggest a few on your own.

- Fred could build a big slingshot and fling himself across the lake.
- Fred *is* a frog and frogs do have long tongues. Fred could climb a tree right next to the mud and stretch out his tongue to grab a limb in the next tree before the bears get him. Then he could swing from tree to tree like Tarzan using his tongue instead of a rope.
- Fred could build a submarine (or an airplane) and cross the lake without the crocodile noticing.
- Fred could dig a tunnel under the lake and walk through the tunnel to the meadow to get the food.
- Etc., Etc. That sort of thing.

With a list of six to a dozen schemes on the board, turn back to the class and ask, "How do we pick which one to use for our story?"

Let the class debate that question for a moment before you bring them back to your partial demonstration of Fred's plan to let the birds carry him across the lake (end of Part 1). The critical bit of information that was going to make that plan work was knowing something about Fred the audience could use to get him into BIG TROUBLE.

How do you pick which plan (or plans) to use? By discovering more about your main character (Big Fred) and by then matching relevant traits of Fred to each potential plan.

You need to create character traits for Fred. To make this process quicker and more productive, you will define each of the categories of information students will invent. But first, give students these three rules.

1. Don't offer any suggestions of traits that would make sense for a frog, that we would expect. (No "he's good at jumping," or "he's afraid of snakes," or "he's green.") Those are what we would expect.

2. In fact, you want just the opposite. You want students to suggest things that make **NO** sense for a frog, that readers would never expect of a frog!

3. Don't offer any suggestions of traits that fit with what we already know about the story. (No "Fred can run faster than a bear," or "Fred can hold his breath for an hour.") We can instantly see how those traits fit with existing information in this story. Bring in new ideas. Don't think about a frog. Think about a character—any character.

I recommend that, one by one, you work through the following categories. Write the category on the board and then say, "I want to know something that Fred is afraid of, or allergic to, good at, etc."

Advice: Work with each suggestion to make it more specific and more extreme and, thereby, more fun. If someone suggests that Fred is afraid of fish, suggest that they pick a specific kind of fish. Then make it a kind of fish Fred should not logically be afraid of (like minnows, or guppies). If someone suggests that Fred is afraid of grass, have him specify the exact kind of grass (bluegrass, crabgrass, etc.).

Encourage creativity here. Applaud and award creativity. Often, suggestions that seem silly when mentioned become the most useful when writing the story. Don't worry about how you will use a suggestion in the story. That consideration comes much later. For now, you want as diverse and imaginative a set of traits on the board as possible for later consideration and use.

Here are the categories I think you should have your class develop (in this order):

- **Fears** (Be sure to include at least one insect, one flower, and one kind of tree.)
- **Allergies** (Be sure to include at least one flower and one kind of tree.)
- **Physical flaws and frailties** (Let them build a long list if they are on a roll.)
- **Things Fred is good at** (Nothing frog-like! If they need help, suggest dancing, cooking, astronomy, cards, banjo playing, welding, etc., etc.)
- **Things Fred is bad at** (Again, allow nothing that is in any way naturally frog-like)
- **Best subjects in school** (These will be key strengths Fred will have to rely on to get out of trouble.)
- **Worst subjects in school** (Having Fred be bad at math, science, spelling, are great ways to get him in trouble.)

This, of course, is a partial list of possible categories of valuable character traits. Still, it will do quite nicely for this story.

Now work with students to match traits with selected possible schemes. Pick a couple of traits that you could use to get Fred into trouble, and a trait or two he could use to escape from that trouble, for each of the listed plans.

A definite six-step pattern for action (event) sequences begins to emerge.

1. Character has a goal and problem.

2. Character creates a plan to overcome problem and reach goal.

3. Use conflicts (bears and crocodile) to create risk and danger for the main character.

4. Plan unravels because of some character trait the character did not adequately consider.

5. Character gets into BIG TROUBLE as things unravel.

6. Character uses some other character trait to barely escape from disaster and winds up back where he started. (For Fred this will be when he escapes back to his lily pad as the three little frogs say, "Ummmmm, 'scuse me, Big Fred. Did you bring us back some food?" And Fred sighs, "No, I didn't. The crocodile (or the bears) almost ate me. I think I have to think about it some more. . . ." "Ummmm. 'Scuse me. If we don't get some food in a hurry, we're going to starve!")

Suggest to the class that you have, collectively, created a working plan for an excellent story in five parts. Find a spot to list these on the board.

Part 1	The story introduction and setup. That is exactly what you created in Part 1 of this workout.
Parts 2, 3, & 4	Three attempts by Fred to get the food that both fail following the six-step pattern you just discussed.
Part 5	Fred's final attempt to get the food. Either this one succeeds (and the frogs get food) or it, too, fails and the frogs starve. This part will include the story's climax and resolution.

There is the plan and outline of a story. Collectively you have already created Part 1. You have created the possible plans and all the needed character traits for Parts 2, 3, 4, and 5. All that is left to do is to write those remaining three parts.

Part 3. Their Turn to Build a Scene

That brings us to Part 3 of Fred du Frog, included here as a separate workout (Workout #8 below) since you can do this same activity based on any story that students have read and understand.

Post-Activity Review and Discussion

This game-format workout is the most effective single vehicle I have ever seen to demonstrate the Eight Essential Elements of story structure and to have students experience the process of creating each of them for a story.

It is my experience that students *will* remember this process and their creative efforts. Refer back to them often and use them both for future writing activity and for story comprehension work.

Workout #8: Your Scene

Quick Summary & Purpose

** **Purpose:** • Develop a feel for creating one individual scene (one event) in a longer story.

Summary: Assuming that students have become intimately familiar with a story, its structure, and its characters (as they have with Fred du Frog—see Workout #7 above), they will be in position to create an event of their own to the plotting sequence of that story.

This workout is primarily designed as a final part (Part 3) of Fred du Frog. However, you can use the same process to have students insert their own scenes into other partially or fully developed stories.

Key Grades

Excellent for all intermediate grades

Time Required

20 to 40 minutes for writing
Extra for any rounds of revision and self- or peer editing you want to include

Introduction

In Workout #7 above, you led your class through the process of defining and outlining a great story: Fred du Frog. This workout represents students' chance to insert their own event creation into that growing story.

The directions below are written for Fred du Frog. You can easily adapt them to other stories.

Directions

Each student will write one attempt by Fred to cross the lake and get the food. Each student's contribution must:

1. Begin with Fred sitting on his lily pad as the three itty-bitty frogs whine that they are about to starve and Fred says, "Boys, I've been thinking 'bout it, and I have a plan. . . ."

2. Describe what happens when Fred picks one of the possible schemes the class identified during Part 2.

3. Follow the six-step pattern established in Part 2 of Fred du Frog.

4. Use the traits for Fred developed during Part 2 of that activity to get him into (and then back out of) BIG TROUBLE.

5. End with Fred scampering back onto his lily pad for safety as the little frogs ask, "Ummmmm, Big Fred, did you bring us back some food?"

Rather than being restrictive for student creativity, these structural mandates allow students to focus on the details and specifics of the events of their story and free them to focus their attention on the character interactions and reactions.

Emphasize for your students that their focus while writing should be on the: Details, details, details—especially on TFFS (see TIP #8). Show us how each character thinks, feels, and reacts to each situation and development.

Writing Format

Top right: student name

Upper left: Identify which of Fred's possible plans for getting food you choose.
Next Line: List Fred's traits you will use to get him into BIG TROUBLE.
Next line: State how Fred will escape from being eaten.

Skip a line.

Create a TITLE for Your Event Contribution to the story of Fred du Frog.

Skip a line.

Write!

Post-Activity Review and Discussion

Two follow-up activities have value. First, allow students to share the events they have created for Fred. Second, review how developing the Eight Essential Elements created a powerful, fun, effective story. Finally, review how important it was to create character (goals, motives, traits, and problems) *before* thinking about action and plotting events.

Quick Summary & Purpose

** **Purpose:** • Create story seeds that both provide a sense of story structure and create an avenue for the writer's own passions to leak into the story characters.

Summary: Creating any seed for a story is good. Creating one that encourages the writer to infuse passion into the main character is better. Creating one that also identifies the beginning and ending spots of the story is best. That's the idea of the Love/Hate game.

Key Grades

Excellent for all grades from 2nd through 6th

Time Required

5 minutes or less per usage

Introduction

One of the most consistent student complaints related to writing is the perpetual whine, "I never know what to write about." There is no way to get started with the writing until the writer knows what she will write about. This workout is designed to take care of that nagging problem.

Directions

This is an exercise students can do on their own. First demonstrate it several times for the class. Have students think of something they hate and how they wish it were different. This is a two-part process, and they must be able to specifically articulate both parts.

Have one volunteer announce what he hates and how he wishes it were different. He must be exactly specific on both counts. Otherwise the story drifts toward being vague, unshaped, and difficult to write. Your job is to help students be specific.

As an example, the conversation (for a potentially *very* difficult topic) might go like this.

Student: I hate my brother.
Teacher: What about him do you hate? Everything, or just some things?
Student: I hate the way he treats me.
Teacher: Do you hate *everything* about the way he treats you, or just some things?
Student: I hate the way he steals my stuff and gets away with it.
Teacher: Which do you hate more? That he steals your stuff, or that he gets away with it?

Student: Both.

Teacher: Pick one for this story.

Student: I hate that he steals my stuff.

Teacher: Great. Now how do you wish he were different?

Hating a brother is far too vague and general to write about in one short story and too vague for an audience to quickly appreciate or empathize with. Hating that a brother steals your stuff is easy to handle. It works because it is specific. Small, specific hates work far better than grand, sweeping ones as writing topics.

You will now have to go through a similar focusing process on how they wish things were different. This one often takes considerable thought. It isn't as easy as it appears. However, if the subject is something the student truly hates, it is probable he has already gone through that thought process and knows exactly how he wishes things actually were.

When you finally arrive at a specific story seed, it might look like: I hate that my brother steals my things and I wish that, whenever he did, it would stick to his fingers so that he couldn't let it go and he'd be caught every time. It could also be as simple as I hate the taste of Brussels Sprouts and wish they tasted like chocolate, or I hate going to school and wish we didn't have to go at all. In fact, the simpler the two aspects of this statement are, the easier it will be to write.

In that one simple step, here is what the student has created for his story:

1. **The beginning condition.** Stories are about struggles, the bigger the better. To make this struggle as big as possible, the student must now exaggerate the condition she *hates* as the opening condition of her story.

   Have the student who suggested the topic think of how to make the thing she hates as bad as possible. Then have the class offer other suggestions.

   For the previous example, the main character might come home from school to find half of his stuff missing, or on successive days, *every one* of the main character's favorite things could turn up missing, including things the child really needs—homework or proof of purchase for some item the store thinks was stolen. For the child who hates the taste of Brussels Sprouts, the worst possible situation would be having to eat them all the time. Have the story start as the family moves to a Brussels Sprouts farm, spends all day growing sprouts, and eats them morning, noon, and night. That's bad!

   The worse, the more exaggerated, the opening conditions, the bigger are the problems and struggles for your students' characters to overcome.

2. **The ending situation.** The story ends when its main character gets exactly what the student wished for as a solution for the thing or situation he hated. That's why students have to be specific in saying how they wish the thing they hate were different. What they wish for becomes the ending point of their story.

3. **The main character's identity and goal.** That one simple statement ("I hate . . . , and I wish it . . .") also locks in the main character (he, she, or it in the story who has this wish) and the goal of that main character. This character will be one the student writer closely identifies with and will strongly visualize.

4. **Main character's attitude and passion.** Finally, by knowing what the main character hates (feels very strongly about), we learn something about the attitude, motive, and personality of this character. When the main character acts in the story, we know why she acts as she does because we know her feelings and her goal. More importantly, the writer shares the hates, wishes, and passions of the main character. Now the student writer's own feelings and energy can pour more directly into the story.

It's a simple way to define a story for your students to write, but it works!

The key to successful use of Love/Hate is guiding students to tightly focused, specific hates. Demonstrate the process; then let them help each other. Help them establish a habit of making themselves be specific before you turn them loose to develop their own themes. No hate or love is too small and petty to make a good story. Many, however, are too large, general, and vague.

Options/Variations

As an alternate to picking something your students hate, have them pick something they love but never get enough of. Interestingly, students are never as enthusiastic for this process as they are for the hate theme. Still, with a moment for thought, they can all identify an appropriate topic. The story now tracks the journey from never getting *any* of this thing the character loves, to getting as much as they want. Roald Dahl's *Charlie and the Chocolate Factory* is a classic example of this story structure.

First/Last:

This is another great story-starter game. It requires you (referee) and three students: two who will create a sentence and one who will serve as scribe and keep track of the sentence.

Say to the two sentence creators, "You two will create—pick one, either the first sentence or the last sentence—of a story each student will then write." Point to one of them. "You will create half of the sentence." Point to the other. "And you will create half of the sentence. Easy" Point back to the first student. "I want you to create just the first word of the (first/last) sentence of our story."

He or she will create only that one word. It must be a word that could plausibly serve as the first word of a grammatically correct English-language sentence. Repeat the chosen word and turn to the second student. "You will now create the second word of our sentence that could plausibly follow after _____ (repeat the first word)."

The second student picks any word as long as it is grammatically plausible in the sentence. You turn back to the first student for the third word, and so forth until one of them opts to put in a period (ending the sentence) instead of a new word. They can only opt for a period if that completes a grammatically correct sentence.

If students try to slip in more than one word at a time (and they often do), reject all of those words and make them come up with a different word for that spot in the sentence.

The third student must write the sentence on the board as it grows as the "official" reference for the sentence.

Each student will now write a short story with that same sentence as his or her first sentence. The sentences are usually funny, often nonsensical, but always great story starters for the class. It is always great fun for all students as they watch the sentence evolve and then as they try to make sense out of it as a starting point for their story. The one rule is that students must actually use that sentence as a reasonable and logical place to start their stories.

If you opt for creating the last sentence, students can start their stories wherever they like, but they must logically work toward that one created sentence as their last sentence. The rule is, then, that the story must make sense with that as the closing sentence.

Post-Activity Review and Discussion

Love/hate themes provide powerful seeds for stories because they supply more than just the starting idea. This technique provides a starting condition, the end of the story, the main character, his or her goal, and a good bit about his or her motives and personality.

Still, this is only a seed. The writer must now develop the rest of the core character information and plotting structure before beginning to write.

The technique is simple. Identify the things students hate or love, exactly how they wish it were different, and then exaggerate the starting condition to make it as bad as possible.

Remember to point out that we care more about characters who care about something. The more *they* care, the more passion they feel and show, the more *we* care about them and their story.

Workout #10: Number Stories

Quick Summary & Purpose

** **Purpose:** • Develop a strong sense of story sequencing and of cause-effect sequencing in students

Summary: The class will create a story. Each student will create and contribute one sentence to that evolving story.

Key Grades

Great with 2nd, 3rd, and 4th grades.

Time Required

30 minutes to launch the story
3 to 5 minutes per day thereafter

Introduction

Group stories are fun. This is a fun, drawn-out class story development workout. It lets each student be the primary story contributor for a day, and still forces the whole class to focus on the creation of an effective story. The class will build a story, one sentence at a time, day by day. The story builds over as many days as there are students in the class.

Directions

This is a good group (progressive) story activity *after* your students already have a feel for the sequencing and general flow of stories and *after* they have had at least some introductory exposure to the key elements of story. (See TIP #5.)

With that caveat, tell the class that you will collectively create a story "by the numbers." Each student draws a number (1 through XX {the number of students}). As a class, you'll agree on three core elements of the story: main character, that character's goal in the story, and the antagonist (the being who most wants to prevent the main character from reaching that goal). (See Workout #6, The BIG Three, for more detail.)

Each student will write one sentence for the story. One sentence is added each day. The student who drew #1 will write the story's first sentence. Student #1 writes that sentence overnight and presents it to the class the next morning. After the class has accepted this sentence, student #2 takes over. Knowing what student #1 wrote, student #2 will create his or her sentence overnight and present it to the class the next morning. And so on through the class and through the story.

From *Writing Workouts to Develop Common Core Writing Skills: Step-by-Step Exercises, Activities, and Tips for Student Success, Grades 2–6* by Kendall Haven. Santa Barbara, CA: Libraries Unlimited. Copyright © 2015.

Beginning the Story

Begin by describing the nature of a progressive group story and the process the class will use.

Next hold the drawing of numbers. Be sure to write down the order as students are prone to lose their number and to forget when it's their turn to create a sentence.

As a class, decide on the main character for this story. In order to keep it a character of interest to all students, use considerable discretion in rejecting student-nominated characters you think might be difficult to work with or that won't produce successful stories.

Once you have a character, collectively decide on that character's goal in this story. **What does he/she need to do or get in this story?** Again, feel free to control the list of possible goals, and to rephrase or amend any nominations in order to make the story creating easier and more successful.

Finally, settle on one main antagonist (the villain, the bad guy, the one character who most wants to keep the main character from reaching the story goal).

Find a place (wall or smart board) to keep the growing story visible and handy over the weeks that it will take to complete it. Write these three key story elements at the top of that space.

One more class discussion and you are ready to go. Discuss what kinds of information typically appear at the beginning of a story (meet the main character; find out what his or her goal and problems are) and at the end of the story (resolve the goal and find out how characters feel about that ending point). In between, characters struggle to try to overcome problems and conflicts to reach their goal. As writers, we don't want to make it easy for our characters. No! We want the characters to have to struggle right up to the very end of the story.

Student #1 is now instructed to arrive at school the next morning with sentence #1 of this story written and ready to be presented to the class.

Review and Acceptance

As part of your morning rituals and patterns, build in time for that day's student to read the sentence. Before the sentence is read, you should read the whole story to that point to the class so that all students are visualizing this spot in the story. Now today's student reads his/her sentence.

Then the class must decide if they will accept that sentence as is. Does it fit in that spot of the story? Does it make sense based on what has already been created? Does it resolve the main character's goal too early? (That must be saved for the last sentence in the story.) The class can discuss and question the author of that sentence. That student can defend and justify why he or she created that sentence. You will guide that discussion.

I suggest that you quickly decide if you think the sentence will work as is and lead the discussion accordingly.

If the sentence is accepted, write it onto that space you are using to build the story. If it is rejected, then (when time permits) you will work with that student during the morning to revise and edit the sentence.

Revised sentences are presented back to the class in the afternoon and then added to the growing story.

Your Role

In addition to your role as discussion moderator and chief scribe for the story, you will hold several other key roles.

- Keep a copy of the growing story on your computer so that you can print the current version to give to the next student to work on overnight.
- Sometime in the afternoon, set aside a few minutes to work with the author of the next sentence. Discuss where the story is and where it seems most likely that it will go. Talk about cause-and-effect sequencing, about character development, and about what might be appropriate to reveal at this time.
- Make sure no one writes their sentence before it is their night to do so. I have found that there are always a few students who get excited on day #1 and write their sentences then even though they might be student #15. Those sentences are always rejected.
- If a sentence is rejected, find a few minutes that morning to work with the student to jointly revise and edit his or her sentence. Schedule a time early enough in the afternoon for the student to read the revised sentence so that you will be able to update your computer file, print out the current story for the next night's student writer, and still find a couple of minutes to briefly discuss with that next student what would be appropriate for his or her sentence.
- This growing story also gives you the perfect opportunity to talk about story sequencing as it twists from sentence to sentence. Given what exists in the story on any given day, what does the class think will happen later—and why?

Post-Activity Review and Discussion

This is a popular Parents' Night show-and-tell item in many classes. I have seen many students—often those who struggle most with writing—proudly pointing out their sentence to their parents during open house evenings.

This emerging story also gives you an excellent opportunity to discuss the Eight Essential Elements of effective narratives with your class. Periodically review (as the story slowly builds) which elements are already woven into the story's text and which are not.

CHAPTER 5

INTERMEDIATE-GRADE WORKOUTS

Workout #11: The What-Makes-It-Real Game

Quick Summary & Purpose

** **Purpose:** • Demonstrate that specific, relevant story details create a sense of reality more than anything else students can put in their story.

Summary: By turning a review of what makes a story sound real into a mystery game, students are compelled to sift through a story for all possible clues without even realizing that they are creating a short list of elements to include in their own stories to make them sound equally real.

Key Grades

Best 5th & 6th. Good 4th. Okay 3rd.

Time Required

15–18 minutes for the game; 15–20 for the follow-up discussion

Introduction

It is a key question: how do authors make their writing *seem* real—whether or not it actually is about real places and events? Every fiction story needs to seem as real to the mind of the reader as if it had actually happened. How do student authors create that kind of "reality" in their writing? That is the focus of this workout.

Directions

Divide the class into groups of either three or four. Give each student a moment to recall a personal (real) story on whatever topic you assign. Use simple, broad topics—something funny that happened to you, or something scary. Even a topic as broad as something that happened in your family will work well.

Three rules:

1. These personal and family stories **MUST** have actually happened.

2. They **MUST** have happened at least three years ago

3. These stories **MUST** *not* have been previously shared with other students in the class.

Each student shares with their group the bare-bones summary of their remembered story. Some students will want to drift into elaborate storytelling here. Don't let them. These should be 20- to 30-second summaries. Give the group a total of two minutes and task them to keep on time. Remind each group not to allow anyone from another group to hear anything they say about these stories.

Only after this time has elapsed, instruct each group to choose one of these stories that they think makes the best story, or the one that is their favorite. They cannot combine stories to create a new super-story. They must pick one of the actual stories told by a group member. Give them 30 seconds to accomplish this.

Proceed only after every group has picked their story. Tell the class that every member of the group must now learn that one story they picked well enough so that they could tell it as if it had happened to them. This means that each group member has to question the person to whom it really happened to uncover the information they will need to tell the story.

At your option, you can prompt them about what kind of information they need to master. When and where did it happen? Who was there? What happened? Why? How did the characters feel? Why? etc.

Be sure to tell them that they may adjust the physical reality of the story to be plausibly consistent with their own history. For example, if the story happened between the teller and a brother, a child who doesn't have a brother could say the story happened with a cousin. Who would know the child doesn't have a male cousin?

If the story happened when the teller lived in Atlanta, and the other students never lived in Atlanta, they can say it happened where they really lived at the appropriate time. If Atlanta were important to the story, they would then say it happened while their family was visiting someone (grandmother, friend, etc.) in Atlanta. Again, who would know it wasn't true?

Give the groups 75 to 90 seconds to gather whatever information they need.

You now pick one group. All the members of that group line up at the front of the class and, one by one, tell the complete story, each claiming as they do that it really did happen to them. Instruct the tellers that their goal is to say and do whatever they have to do to convince every person in the room that the story really *did* happen to them. That's their job.

The job of the audience is to figure out to whom it really happened. Don't allow any pause for discussion between tellers. As soon as teller #1 finishes, say, "And now the story from teller #2."

As soon as all the tellers have finished and the thunderous applause has died away, have the audience vote by show of hands for the teller they think the story really happened to. Do not allow any discussion before this vote. Every student must vote.

Usually the biggest vote-getter is not the person to whom the story really happened.

Post-Activity Review and Discussion

This is a fun game and does develop oral storytelling skills. But the real value of this exercise comes from the following discussion. Ask the class, "Why did you vote the way you voted? It doesn't matter if you voted for the right person or not. I still want to know why you thought one story sounded more real than the others."

Write the responses you get on the board, spatially dividing them into two groups: those comments that relate to the story and those that relate to the way the story was told.

Discuss those elements that made the story seem real enough to vote for. Those are extremely powerful story elements for each student to remember to include in their stories.

As you repeatedly use this exercise, vary the story theme. Any commonly available experience will do—summer vacation, time they were scared, something that happened on a bike, disasters with a pet (theirs or someone else's), etc.

Amazingly, I find that every audience votes for the same few reasons. It doesn't much matter if they are 1st graders or teachers, 5th graders or college seniors. Even more amazing, almost all groups mention their reasons for voting in the same order.

First is always *details* in the story. One teller included more details and his story sounded more real. One teller included impossible or unlikely details and so sounded less real. Details create reality.

The second aspect mentioned usually has to do with the *way* the story was told. One teller over-acted, or hesitated and seemed to be making it up. One teller put more expression in the story, or seemed more confident and so was more believable. One seemed more natural and relaxed. One seemed stiffer and more halting. The general impression created by the way the teller told the story seemed more real or less real and so he or she was voted either for or against.

Next mentioned is usually something about characters and the amount of character information one person included. Next is usually humor. Make a list of all the reasons your students mention. It will be a very short list. There are not many things an audience needs in order to enjoy a story.

What makes a story enjoyable are the same few elements that make it sound real. Alone at the top of these lists are story details and that the teller seemed comfortable with, and enthused about, his or her own story.

Workout #12: BIG Trouble!

Quick Summary & Purpose

** **Purpose:** • Develop a sense of character and character reaction.
  • Develop a feel for pre- and post-event descriptive power.
  • Develop a good feel for momentary character sensory perceptions.

Summary: Each student writes a short in-class essay that starts with them getting into BIG TROUBLE. This writing develops their ability to create character and to succinctly link cause-and-effect time sequencing in their writing.

Key Grades

Best: 4th, 5th & 6th. Good: 3rd.

Time Required

30 minutes on day 1 for the writing. 30 to 45 on day 2 for sharing and review.

Introduction

This is one of the most fun writing assignments students ever receive. They can all relate to it and are energized to pour some effort into their writing. The learning comes both from this exuberant writing effort and from the sharing and analysis of the sensory details that build a real, engaging, and credible scene.

Directions

Stand in front of the class with a large open surface (desk or table) in front of you. Say these words and, at the indicated moment, slam you hand (open, palm down) hard on that open surface. The more noise from this slam, the better.

"You walk home, happy, content. All is right with the world. You think nothing can go wrong. You step up onto your front porch. You smile and open the door .... And, WHAM!!!!! (slam here) instantly you perceive that you are in BIG trouble (B-I-G trouble).

The Actual Assignment: *Write the story that begins at that moment. How do you know you're in trouble? What do you think, sense, feel, say, do? Explain—going forward and backwards—from that moment of revelation, to make it a story.*

Now let them write.

From *Writing Workouts to Develop Common Core Writing Skills: Step-by-Step Exercises, Activities, and Tips for Student Success, Grades 2–6* by Kendall Haven. Santa Barbara, CA: Libraries Unlimited. Copyright © 2015.

They must start just where you started: with themselves happily approaching their own front door without a care in the world. After establishing that wonderful moment when they realize that they are in BIG TROUBLE, they can back fill as needed to develop the situation, and move forward toward resolution of the event.

I typically give intermediate grades 30 to 40 minutes to write. I have found that all students—even the most reluctant writers—respond enthusiastically to this writing prompt.

Post-Activity Review and Discussion

Read all student's writing overnight, and select three or four to be read to the class. Let these students read their own writing out loud the next day.

Guide any follow-up discussion to two topics:

1. The sensory detail at the moment the front door is opened. Note how those pieces that really suck listeners in provide detailed information about what the student at the door saw, heard, felt, sensed, and otherwise perceived. (See TIP #8: TFSS.)

2. Detailed and believable pre- and post-moment descriptions. That is, effective writing sets listeners up for the key moments and then allows us to watch the aftermath of those moments.

I prefer not to grade this activity. However, if grades are to be assigned, they should be based on the depth and breadth of detail used to describe the moment of realization after opening the front door, and on the character development in the pre- and post-revelation development of the complete story.

There is no absolute need to have students rewrite their essays. However, following class discussion, this is a good opportunity to allow students to revise, edit, and *then* rewrite their essay.

Workout #13: How to Make a Better Peanut Butter & Jelly Sandwich

Quick Summary & Purpose

** **Purpose:** • Develop an awareness of the need for precision in writing description.
   • Develop a feel for the persuasive power of detailed imagery and the dual need for evocative sensory description combined with precise physical detail in order to build vivid, alluring, engaging, and powerful images in readers' minds.
   • Appreciate the process and power of adding details during revision and editing.

Summary: All they have to do is write down directions for making a better peanut butter & jelly sandwich. However, students will quickly become aware of the extent to which they write for themselves (and what *they* know) and not for the readers (and what *they* know). They will also clearly see the power of sensory images and details to guide readers' interpretation of their writing.

Key Grades

GREAT for all intermediate grades!

Time Required

3rd & 4th grade: 30 minutes each day for three days. 5th & 6th: 20 minutes each day for three days. For all grades 30 minutes for a review and discussion on day 4.

Introduction

This is a three-step writing workout. Do not reveal that future steps even exist until they are actually being assigned.

Directions

Step 1: The Basics

The Assignment

By the numbers, write detailed directions for making the best-ever PB&J sandwich.

That's the assignment. If they ask for clarification, say that you want them to write down in exact sequential order each step for making what they think is the ideal (the best) peanut butter & jelly sandwich. Yes, they can (even should) number the steps as they write them.

That should be sufficient. Have them double space when they write these directions.

From *Writing Workouts to Develop Common Core Writing Skills: Step-by-Step Exercises, Activities, and Tips for Student Success, Grades 2–6* by Kendall Haven. Santa Barbara, CA: Libraries Unlimited. Copyright © 2015.

Students must save all of their writing for this activity. They will write their directions three times. The most powerful teaching will come at the end when they compare the three versions.

Invariably, someone will claim to hate PB&J sandwiches. For them, the best PB&J is the one you make and then throw away. But they still have to write directions for making that sandwich first. Instead of eating the sandwich as the final direction, these writers will instruct readers to throw it in the garbage and eat something else.

Evaluation and Post Discussion

Overnight, look *very literally* at what each student has written and try to identify the unstated assumptions each has made. Identify as many of these on each student's page as you can. Don't grade the papers at this point. Comment only on—but profusely on—the imprecision of their directions.

Many, for example, will say to get the peanut butter out of the refrigerator and spread it on the bread without instructing you to close the refrigerator, unscrew the lid of the peanut butter jar, get a spreading knife (or table knife) from the silverware drawer, and to use that knife to do the scooping and spreading. Many will omit telling you where to place the bread once you have retrieved it from its wrapper (on the counter? on the floor? in the sink? etc.).

Be as picky as you dare, based on the writing competency level of your students.

Next day, you will need to bring to school a loaf of bread, a jar of peanut butter, and several knives (including at least one that would not work well at all for use in making a peanut butter & jelly sandwich).

Return the papers; give students a chance to look over all of your notes and marks; and then start a discussion with this live demonstration:

Find one of their papers that mentioned neither taking the bread out of the loaf wrapper nor unscrewing the jar of peanut butter. (A typical direction says, "Put the bread on a plate and put the peanut butter on it with a knife.")

Read such a direction and, as you do, place the entire loaf of bread on a plate (unopened) and place the jar of peanut butter (unopened) and a knife on top of it. You have accurately and literally followed their direction. Ask the class if you have now successfully made a PB&J sandwich.

As an alternative, students rarely provide specific details on how to assemble the sandwich once peanut butter has been spread on one piece of bread and jelly on the other. Most say, "Put the two pieces together." Fine. For your demo, slap the bread together with the jelly and peanut butter on the outside.

You get the idea of the demo. Do as many as you want. Literally and exactly follow a student's written directions to demonstrate the lack of precise and complete details. These demos are fun to watch and graphically point out the serious lackings in the level of detail students provided.

Now launch a discussion along these core themes:

1. The Curse of Knowledge. Each student already holds a detailed mental image of each step. *Any* words they write will pull that picture into their minds and *seem* to be totally adequate. Whatever they write will make perfect sense to them—because they already know! The "trick" to successful writing is figuring out what you have to write so that someone who doesn't already know will form the same mental images that you already hold.

2. What do the readers really need? Why can't they see it as well as you? Discuss what information (in general) readers need in order to form vivid, interesting mental images. Have students try to identify (from their own reading experience) what pops rich and engrossing pictures into their minds while they read.

Step 2: Give Me Details or Give Me Reading Death!

The Assignment

It's time to rewrite their directions. The next page presents a feedback sheet I have used to help 3rd through 6th graders think of additional relevant details to include. It is not essential to hand this sheet out. But I find that it always helps when I do.

Rewrite your directions, being clear and precise so that anyone will be able to follow them and successfully make a PB&J sandwich.

Use the same time limit as before. No other directions or discussion should be needed.

Step 2 Editing Notes

Making a Peanut Butter & Jelly Sandwich

You have written the basics. That's good. Now it's time to make your writing sparkle! It's time to "**Do the DETAILS!**"

Here are questions to think about when you write a 2nd draft.

1. "Get out" from *where*? "Put" the bread, jelly, etc. *where*?

2. What kind of bread do you think is best? Why?

3. Do you prefer smooth or crunchy peanut butter?

4. What is your favorite kind of jelly? Why?

5. How thick do you spread the peanut butter and jelly on?

6. Do you wipe off the knife after spreading peanut butter? Do you lick it clean? Do you smear some peanut butter into the jelly jar?

7. Sensory details: What does each ingredient smell like? Look like? Feel like?

8. Scenic details: add scenic details so that I can accurately picture you making the sandwich in whatever room you make it in.

9. Where and how do you eat the sandwich?

10. Is there any essential cleanup? Describe it.

Evaluation & Post Discussion

Again overnight, read these version 2 directions to make sure that they have significantly increased the specificity of, and level of, detail in their directions. There is no need to comment back to each student on this version. In this version, they typically focus on physical, factual details. These often read as if the student were giving directions to a robot. However, in so doing, they typically overlook describing their sensory experience and reaction to the process and to their sandwich. The writing is usually much more accurate. But it is not engaging, not compelling, and is, well, typically boring.

Lead a short in-class discussion on what makes a narrative exciting and fun to read. It is not the action (in this case, their culinary directions). It is the character and sensory detail that places vivid images in our minds and sets us up to be excited by the other elements in a story.

Step 3. The Sales Pitch

The Assignment

Time for the students to make one final rewrite of their directions. The goal of this rewrite is to move from precision to engaging and persuasive.

Rewrite your directions one more time. In this rewrite, convince me that yours is the best, the most delicious, mouth-watering PB&J recipe in the world. Convince me that I should pick your PB&J directions as my all-time favorite meal, as my mouth-watering ideal. Convince me that I will adopt your directions as the only way I will ever again want to prepare a PB&J sandwich.

They write their directions a third time, focusing this time not on the factual directions—supposedly already there—but on the reader's sensory experience of both the process and the product.

I often hand students a second version of the step 2 handout—one that includes additional sensory cueing.

Step 3 Editing Notes

Making a Peanut Butter & Jelly Sandwich

You have written the basics. That's good. Now it's time to make your writing sparkle! It's time to "**Do the DETAILS!**"

Here are questions to think about when you write a second draft.

1. "Get out" from *where*? "Put" the bread, jelly, etc. *where*?

2. What kind of bread do you think is best? Why?

3. Do you prefer smooth or crunchy peanut butter?

4. What is your favorite kind of jelly? Why?

5. How thick do you spread the peanut butter and jelly on?

6. Do you wipe off the knife after spreading peanut butter? Do you lick it clean? Do you smear some peanut butter into the jelly jar?

7. Sensory details: What does each ingredient smell like? Look like? Feel like?

8. Scenic details: add scenic details so that I can accurately picture you making the sandwich in whatever room you make it in.

9. Where and how do you eat the sandwich?

10. Is there any essential cleanup? Describe it.

11. What does the sandwich remind you of?

12. What does it feel like, smell like, and taste like in your hands and in your mouth? Is it messy or neat to eat? Does the jelly ooze out the side and trickle down your fingers and arm? What does it sound like as you bite into the sandwich and chew each bite?

13. Hunt for GREAT action verbs to describe each step and action in the process (ones like smear, smoosh, glob, smother, slap, or slather instead of dull ones like "put").

14. You are allowed **only one** "put" and one "get" in your directions. Find better verbs for all of the others.

15. Double space (write on every other line).

Post-Activity Review and Discussion

Both you and each student should compare the three versions. Which is the most fun to read? Which engages you and holds your attention? Look at powerful, forceful words and images in version #3 compared to the bland and uninteresting words in version #1. Now revisit the discussion on what builds a vivid image. What makes you want to read something? What holds your attention?

While you can grade either the quality of each student's version #3 writing or (I think preferably) the improvement from version #1 to version #3, I think this is best kept as an ungraded—but powerful—demonstration of students' natural writing style (version #1) and the impact of focused revision and editing (version #3).

Workout #14: My Favorite Season

Quick Summary & Purpose

** **Purpose:** • Learn the advantages of oral development of details and personal positions.
• Learn the persuasive power of relevant sensory details

Summary: This workout is couched as a class debate/discussion about which is the "best" season. Students are required to take a stance and justify their choice both verbally (in small groups) and in writing. The format allows them to watch how the quality and persuasiveness of their writing grows over the course of each step.

Key Grades

Excellent for 3rd through 6th.

Time Required

Step 1: 10 minutes
Step 2: 15 to 20 minutes
Step 3: 30 minutes
Discussion: 15 to 30 minutes

Introduction

Through a long series of student interviews, I have found that students see events they write about much more clearly, and in much more detail, in their minds than they ever put on the page when they write. I have found that the problem is that they begin to write before they have fully and concretely developed their mental images. Thus, the writing reflects this mental fuzziness.

This is an activity designed to show students how much easier it is to write compelling imagery and arguments if they first take the time to orally develop and refine those images in their own minds.

Directions

This is a three-step exercise.

Step 1. The Initial Writing

Have students decide which of the four basic seasons is their favorite (spring, summer, fall, or winter) and write down three or four reasons for why it is their favorite. They must save these pieces of paper.

From *Writing Workouts to Develop Common Core Writing Skills: Step-by-Step Exercises, Activities, and Tips for Student Success, Grades 2–6* by Kendall Haven. Santa Barbara, CA: Libraries Unlimited. Copyright © 2015.

Step 2. The Oral Arguments

Designate one of the four corners of the room for each season, and instruct everyone to go to the corner that corresponds to their favorite.

The group of students clustered in each corner must first identify one student as discussion leader and one student as group spokesperson. The leader will be charged to lead a group discussion during which that group of students will lay out all of the reasons why their chosen season is the best and should be picked as *everybody's* favorite.

The spokesperson must take notes and be prepared to orally argue why their season is the best.

I usually give groups five minutes to accomplish this organization and compilation of their arguments. I often circulate to those groups with the fewest students to make sure they have strong arguments for why their season is the best.

Now, one at a time, the spokesperson for each season steps forward and presents his or her arguments. You act as debate moderator. After each season's spokesperson has presented his or her case, allow the spokesperson for each of the other three seasons to offer one—only one—argument for why he or she *doesn't* like the season of the spokesperson who just presented.

Allow no other discussion or side comments during these oral arguments.

Step 3.

Students return to their seats. They will now write a persuasive essay arguing that everyone should agree with their pick of the best season.

Before they are allowed to write, they should look at (and revise if they want to) their list of reasons why their pick is the best season.

Having revised that list, they should turn two of their reasons into activities (**things to do** that are representative of their reasons why this is the best season). Have students draw a quick picture of each of these two activities. Technically, these are visual notes.

Finally, having heard from advocates of the other seasons, each student should write down one reason why he or she *doesn't like* each of the other three seasons.

Now—and only now—they are ready to write a persuasive essay arguing for why their season is the best. In that essay they will describe in vivid, compelling detail those two chosen activities and will include their reasons for disliking the other three seasons.

Post-Activity Review and Discussion

Students can now compare that first piece of paper listing their three or four reasons for choosing one season to their final essay.

Discuss with the class what benefit they gained from the time spent on oral argument and on sketching those two pictures. Create first; write second.

Workout #15: Three Interesting Things

Quick Summary & Purpose

** **Purpose:** • Learn how to make story characters interesting to readers.
• Experience the failure of vague and general character description to engage and interest readers.

Summary: Students tend to write vague, general character descriptions. This is a workout to make that writing problem clear and conscious. Students will attempt to write interesting descriptions of three characters and, through the reactions they receive from fellow students, will learn exactly what is—and is not—interesting to readers.

Key Grades

Excellent for 4th through 6th. Good for 3rd.

Time Required

15 minutes for the writing
20 to 30 minutes for the activity and discussion

Introduction

Readers are supposed to synthesize the specific bits of character detail provided by the writer into general conclusions ("He is funny," She is a liar," "He is good at sports," etc.). That's a reader's job. When students flip roles to become writers, they tend to carry that same old job with them. They write in general character conclusions ("He is weird," "She is nice," etc.).

This workout is designed to make them aware that, as writers, their job is to provide the specifics and let their readers do the synthesis work.

Directions

Each student needs a piece of paper. Along the left-hand margin they write "Family"; then indent below it and, on three successive lines, write 1, 2, and 3. Below that they write "Other" along the margin and again indent below it and write 1, 2, and 3. Drop down and write "Me" along the margin and 1, 2, and 3 below that.

From *Writing Workouts to Develop Common Core Writing Skills: Step-by-Step Exercises, Activities, and Tips for Student Success, Grades 2–6* by Kendall Haven. Santa Barbara, CA: Libraries Unlimited. Copyright © 2015.

Their paper now looks like this:

Family

1

2

3

Other

1

2

3

Me

1

2

3

You now instruct each student to select one family member.

Rules: It must be a person (no pets), but not the student him- or herself. It can be any relative (living or dead) as long as the student writer has actually met this person.

Students will now write three things (factual bits of information) about this selected family member that they think are interesting on lines 1, 2, & 3 under "Family." Each item must be written in one sentence. Every statement must be true and accurate. Anything can qualify for inclusion as long as the student thinks it is something interesting about this specific person.

If students seem truly stuck, discuss possible categories of information as a class: physical traits, their history, possessions, hobbies or jobs, abilities and talents, disabilities, fears, hopes and dreams, friends and acquaintances, accomplishments . . . literally *anything* might make this person interesting.

Give students only a couple of minutes to write these three sentences.

Writing Rule: Students may *NOT* name the person in any of these three sentences. Use only third-person pronouns: "he" and "she."

Move to the next category, "Other." Students do the same thing, following the same rules for a person they know who is *not* related to them in any way.

Remind them that they may not name the person. Use only third-person pronouns "he" and "she."

Finally, now that they are getting used to writing interesting traits, they will write three things about themselves that they think would be interesting to a stranger meeting them for the first time.

Writing Rule: Students may *NOT* use "I" for any of these three sentences even though they are all about the student who is writing them. If the student is a girl, she writes "she." If a boy, write, "he." Use only third-person pronouns: "he" and "she."

I recommend that you do not model effective character description statements at this time. Students will simply all mimic what you said or wrote. However, for your use in guiding them to creating something to write down, here are a few common examples of ineffective and more effective description.

Note that the effective wording is always specific, vivid, and emphasizes what is different and unique about the character using images and terms that are (hopefully) a bit unusual.

Ineffective	Effective
He is funny.	He once made my grandmother laugh so hard she peed her pants.
She travels a lot.	She has been to all 50 states and to 11 foreign countries
He is good at sports.	He set a school record for both the 110-meter hurdles and the high jump.
She plays funny instruments.	She is so good at playing the harmonica with her nose that she was invited to play for the school board.
He does weird stuff.	He can write forward and backwards, and he plays spoons with his feet.

In-Class Analysis

Each student has now written nine character trait statements that they think are interesting (three each about three different people). Have students pick the three of those nine individual statements that they think are their three most interesting individual statements. It doesn't matter who these statements are about. These are simply what the student thinks are the three most interesting statements they wrote. (Could be two about one person and one about another. Could be one about each person. Doesn't matter.)

Students should star these three picks in the left-hand margin.

Now you need volunteers who will stand up and read those three starred statements. The class must focus not on the person, but on one, simple question: is this character trait statement interesting to me or not?

Here are the rules:

1. While reading, the student may not—even if asked—identify the person being described.

2. You want all three statements to sound the same so that students focus on the description. To do that, the reader will shift the gender of all three statements to his or her own gender no matter who the statements are about. If a boy gets up to read his three sentences, he will always use "he"—even if the statement is about his mother, sister, or aunt. If a girl gets up, she will always use "she"—again, even if the statement is about a male relative.

3. The first volunteer reads all three statements with no comment or discussion. Then have that student repeat the first statement. Have the class vote: It is interesting to me (thumbs up); it isn't interesting (thumbs down); or it's in-between (wiggling horizontal thumb).

4. Ask the class why they voted as they did. Make them be specific in justifying their vote. During this discussion the volunteer student may not add additional detail. Not yet.

5. Ask those who voted thumbs down or wiggly-horizontal thumb what they would do to make this statement more interesting. (Yes, you will now probably traipse into the realm of fiction. But that is alright for this activity.) Work with the class to make this one statement more interesting. Compare the idea behind each of their suggestions for how to improve the original statement with the qualities of effective character detail listed in the Post-Activity Discussion section.

6. Shift to the volunteer's second statement and repeat. If one of this student's statements seems tailor-made for rapid improvement (or, conversely, seems truly interesting), single that one statement out for class analysis.

7. Shift to another volunteer reader.

As you work through half-a-dozen statements that the class works to improve, watch for trends and patterns in how they make the sentences more interesting. Those will form a key part of the post-activity discussion and teaching.

Post-Activity Review & Discussion

Over the course of this workout you and your students will have used the important characteristics of interesting (effective) description as they work to create interesting character descriptions.

Good description is:

- **Specific** (as opposed to "general" and—more importantly—as opposed to "conclusion statements" about the character)

- **Unusual** (atypical characteristics, comparisons, or descriptors are always more interesting)
- **Unique** (a primary purpose of character traits is to differentiate this character from all others. Effective details show how this character is *different*.)
- **Vivid** (character description that includes the sensory information that lets a reader form vivid mental imagery is always more interesting. The key word for creating vivid mental images is *sensory information*.)

Workout #16: One-Sided Conversation

Quick Summary & Purpose

** **Purpose:** • Learn the art of writing effective dialogue for their characters.
• Learn the elements of effective character voice.

Summary: This is a fun game that focuses on one question: What does revealing and engaging character dialogue look like?

Key Grades

Best: 5th & 6th. Good 4th.

Time Required

Setup & Opening Discussion: 15 minutes
Writing: 15 to 20 minutes
Sharing & Discussion: 15 to 20 minutes
Optional Compression: 15 to 20 minutes (plus another 15 for sharing)

Introduction

One of the character traits that most quickly and easily makes a character interesting is to give that character a voice, and to make that voice distinctive. Yet that is not an easy thing for most students to do.

A voice is a combination of what a person says (his dialogue) and how he says it. Each person's voice is strongly influenced by his physical characteristics, history, social environment, family, personality, current emotional state, and by the situation.

But beyond just having voice and dialogue reveal information about the character, that dialogue must keep a story moving. And that is the second difficult aspect to writing character dialogue. Student writers tend to write dialogue that either reveals character or moves the story forward, but not both. Yet their dialogue *must* do both! This workout will definitely help.

Directions

This is a fun activity to use anytime to refresh your students' skills in creating effective character voice and dialogue.

Give your students the basic definition of "voice:" *a combination of what a character says and how he or she says it*. Then begin with this class discussion question: What would make one person's voice different from another's?

From *Writing Workouts to Develop Common Core Writing Skills: Step-by-Step Exercises, Activities, and Tips for Student Success, Grades 2–6* by Kendall Haven.
Santa Barbara, CA: Libraries Unlimited. Copyright © 2015.

Let the class offer their ideas. Keep a list of their valid offerings on the board. Prompt them as needed to get them to identify at least the elements of this basic list: gender, physical size, age, regional accent and vocabulary, family, education, personality, current emotional state, the audience (the person/group to whom you are speaking).

Each of these character elements could make one person's voice significantly different from another's. Each of these elements is also a valuable tool to help students imagine a voice for a character they create. They will need to use this list in a few minutes.

Describe the following situation for your students, and be sure they are clear on the concept before proceeding to the actual activity.

Imagine sitting in a room with someone who is talking on the telephone. You hear only one side of the conversation—only what the person says who is sitting in the room with you, talking on the phone. You never hear what the person on the other end of the line says. Your students are going to create and write just that one side of a conversation—just as if they wrote down only what the person they're listening to said during a telephone conversation.

First, ask the class what they need to know in order to be able to write this dialogue. Let them flounder for a bit trying to identify what they need. For every request other than the following three, tell the class that they must each make that element up on their own. The three key story elements the class must agree on and ***all use*** are:

1. The fictional human character (the *main character*) whose words (dialogue) each student will write. Let class members offer suggestions, and have the class vote on their favorite. Create just a name, gender, and age for this character. (Example: *Max is a 15-year-old boy.*) You serve as both moderator and censor. Instantly reject anything that you think will be difficult for your students to work with. Reject all nonfictional characters and all fictional characters that have already been created and used.

2. Who this character is talking to over the telephone (the *antagonist*). (Example: *Max's mother.*) Again, let the students offer nominations and then vote.

3. What the main character needs from the other person during this conversation (a *goal*). (Example: *Max wants permission to stay out until 1:30 AM on a school night.*)

Each student will then individually create the following for their own version of this conversation:

1. A specific voice for the main character.

2. Two reasons why the person on the other end of the phone line ***doesn't*** want to give the main character what he or she wants (*conflict*).

3. Why the main character desperately needs that goal (*motive*).

An example of the format they should use is shown below. "————" is used to show when the person on the other end of the telephone is talking. Students will, of course, have to imagine exactly what the other person says during this conversation. However they will not write what the other persons says and will not later share it with the class.

They will write only one side of this conversation, recording only what the main character (the person they are supposedly sitting next to) actually says.

Example One-Sided Conversation

Background Information

Character: _____ *Steve, a 16-year-old boy (S)* _____

Other Person he/she is talking to: _____ *his grandmother (G)* _____

Goal: _____ *talk Granny into buying Steve a new car* _____

Motive: ___ *He thinks he'll look cool and he's tired of his parents driving him on dates.* ___

Key traits of this character's voice: ___ *Steve is hesitant and" ummm's" and " uuuuh's" a lot.* _____

Other Person's two reasons for not giving the main character what he/she wants.

1. Steve has already had two accidents while driving on his learner's permit. _____

2. Steve's grades are way below the "C" average he was supposed to maintain in order to get his license. _____

One-Sided Conversation: (S: marks when Steve talks and what he says. G: marks where Granny talks. Students write "———" to mark where Granny talks since they may not write her actual words).

S: Ummm, Hi, Granny. Whatcha doin'?

G: ———

S: Your poker club? Sure hope you, ahhh, win lots of money.

G: ———

S: Well, see, ummm. It's almost my birthday—my 16th birthday.

G: ———

S: No, next week, Granny. Cathy's birthday is in January.

G: ———

S: Well, anyway, uuuum, I know what I, ahhh, want you to get for my present this year. See, I, ummmmm need some wheels.

G: ———

S: Not a bicycle, Granny. A car.

G: ———

S: I don't want you to give me a ride. You have to . . . well, ummm, buy me a new car.

G: ———

S: Granny? . . . Ummmm, Granny! Stop laughing like that. I'm serious.

G: ———

S: I only had two accidents. And they weren't my fault. And, ahhhh, besides, they don't count 'cause it wasn't my car.

G: ———

S: I know that's what we said. But, ahhh, my grades are almost a C average.

G: ———

S: Well, that's only one-and-a-half grades below a C average . . . .

G: ———

And so on.

Have students use this format to write their one-sided conversation. They may only write the actual words their main character says. Their goals as they write are to:

- Make their character interesting,
- Present a clear and consistent voice for this character that will give readers a good sense of the character's personality and emotions,
- Reveal the conflict between the main character and the other person as well as that other person's reasons for not wanting to give in to the main character,
- Show exactly how the conversation (conflict) ends (resolution).

After everyone has written their conversation, allow volunteers to read what they have written to the class. The reader should *not* read the antagonist's reasons for not wanting to do as the main character wants. The class should be able to deduce them from the dialogue.

Students should read the dialogue *in character voice*, pausing during those times when the antagonist is speaking. Briefly discuss the voices they created for their characters and how their dialogues revealed the key information they were assigned to include.

Option: Story Compression

You will find that most students make virtually every statement by the main character wordy and longer than it needs to be. The solution: "Compression."

Have students rewrite their One-Sided Conversation. However, put an upper limit on the number of words that character is allowed to say each time he/she speaks. The most common word limits are either nine words or seven words.

As students rewrite their dialogue, they must search for ways to provide the same information using fewer words in order to comply with the compression word limit.

Have several volunteers read both the original and the compressed versions. In most cases you will find that compression increases the emotional power and the excitement of the conversation—important characteristics of effective dialogue.

Post-Activity Review and Discussion

Dialogue carries great energy and reveals character. With practice, every student can create consistently effective dialogue. Dialogue is worth practicing because it is such a valuable way to create interest in a character. The key to creating dialogue is to first create a clear voice for each character. How does he talk? What does he say? How does he say it?

Effective dialogue must also convey important story information, moving the story forward while it reveals character. The more students study dialogue when they read and the more they practice writing it, the better theirs will become.

Quick Summary & Purpose

** Purpose: • Learn to weave factual information into a strong, character-based story development and writing.

Summary: This is a different format for a research-written report. The idea is to provide greater motive for student research efforts, and to make the writing much more fun. This is a way to blend the fun and writing control of fiction with factual research.

Key Grades

Excellent for 3rd through 6th

Time Required

Rather than being a separate activity, assigning *por qua* stories is part of existing student research, study, and writing work. No extra time is required. However, most teachers create (and students eagerly want) specific blocks of time at the end for students to share their creations.

Introduction

This activity is designed to be used as part of a factual curriculum research effort (typically either for science or history class—but certainly not limited to those two). I have seen classes create wonderful *por qua* stories after studying aspects of space, geography, the environment, American history, etc.

"*Por qua*" literally translates as "for why." *Por qua* stories explain why things are as they are. Many of Rudyard Kipling's stories serve as *por qua* stories. So do many of the stories from Native American cultures.

Por qua stories are fun. They provide fictional characters and fictional histories to explain why things are as we currently find them to be: why the beaver has a flat tail, why the planets circle the sun, why the skunk has a white stripe, why there are tides in the ocean, why the ocean is salty, why the land is shaped as it is, why rivers run to the sea. Any possible "why" question can be answered by a *por qua*–formatted story.

Por qua stories are good choices for student writing because they feature simple, easy story structures. The main character has a flaw or a discontent that causes him/her to upset the "normal" status quo. All the characters around this main character react—generally quite negatively. Conflicts, problems, and struggles ensue. Things end up with a new "normal"—what we experience today.

This structure gives students a chance to let their imaginations fly! It also forces them to develop and rely on character elements more than plotting—an excellent writing habit to develop for all forms and genres of writing.

And those stories are always fun! Fun to read and fun to write. The idea of this exercise is to use the fun and enjoyment of a *por qua* format to let students research and explain actual natural phenomena.

Directions

Read several *por qua* stories that explain phenomena within the general subject that your class is studying. Discuss the form, character development, and plotting patterns.

As the class studies some unit for which they will write a *por qua* story, have each student pick one specific subject-related phenomenon he or she wants to write about. This should come to you for your approval in the form:

"I will explain why the _____ came to be (or is as we now see it)."

Make sure that each chosen phenomenon is sufficiently specific so that it will be easy to write about and also will allow the student to incorporate significant study information.

After you approve the topic phenomenon, students need to create the characters, goals, motives, problems, and struggles of their story. All *por qua* stories end with the physical reality we actually see around us. Use the *Por Qua* Story Planning Sheet (next page) or design your own. Completing this type of form forces students to plan their story (Effective Writing Step #1) before they begin to write.

Once you approve their planning sheet, students are turned loose to write their stories. While writing, they may not violate known factual information—known science or history. Rather, successful *por qua* stories use as much factual information as possible in weaving their fictional explanations.

Por Qua ("For Why?") Story Planning Sheet

Title:

Phenomenon I will explain: Why the _____ came to be the way it is today.

How things are at the Beginning:

How things are at the End:

My Main Character:

Key Flaw (What gets this character in trouble):

Other interesting character traits I'll use for this character:

How "normal" is disturbed:

Other central characters (and their defining characteristics):

Key story events:

Post-Activity Review and Discussion

This is an excellent writing assignment for the inclusion of a formal revision step. When they turn in their papers, don't worry about spelling, grammar, and punctuation. Not yet. First revise. Does the story make sense? Do the characters seem interesting, and do their actions explain the phenomenon supposedly being explained? Is there a climax moment/scene in the story? Do you clearly see main character goals and motives? Can you suggest ways to make the story more fun and clever?

Now let students take those notes and revisions. I like to give these notes and ideas to students in live, one-on-one discussions rather than as written notes.

Collect the revised papers and now conduct a line-editing review. This is the time for spelling, grammar, etc. checks and corrections. Be sure to tell students what each of these steps is for and why you are separating revision from editing. (There is no need to check spelling in paragraphs that will be rewritten (or cut) during revision. Once students edit, they tend to be far less willing to revise.)

Finally, let students share their work. Use their stories to launch a discussion about what elements create fun, captivating, interesting *por qua* stories.

Workout #18: Dollars for Details

Quick Summary & Purpose

** **Purpose**: • Develop both a strong feel for effective details and a motive for seeking them out each time students write.

Summary: This is a fun, rewarding, and inexpensive way to encourage students to hunt for effective details and descriptions and to develop an appreciation for the value and benefit of effective detail writing.

Key Grades

Excellent for all intermediate grades

Time Required

No more than 5 minutes when added onto existing writing assignments

Introduction

Details are the critical element for creating reader interest. We create stories, but we write details. Details about the characters, about the scenes, about the events and actions create all of the vivid images that form in readers' minds. We reveal all of the key informational elements by writing details. Effective details are essential for all forms and genres of writing.

Yet it has been my experience that student writers don't naturally develop the habit of creating and using effective details. It has to be a conscious effort.

Effective details are specific, unusual, unique (different), and use sensory information to create vivid mental images. (See the discussion section of Workout #15, "Three Interesting Things.")

I have found that occasionally putting a cash value on the most vivid, graphic, gripping detailed description developed during any writing assignment motivates all students to think details!

Directions

When assigning any piece of writing to your students, announce that this will be a "Dollars for Details" assignment.

Student writing proceeds normally. While you are later reading, assessing, and grading, you are also screening for stand-out, vivid, strong bits of detail. Select two or three that you like the best. (But don't select any that you don't think are exemplary. Better to have no awards than to give out an award for work that doesn't merit it.)

Before returning these papers, announce the "Dollars for Details" winners. Read the winning detail; read it again within the context of the sentence in which it appears; and explain why it merits a prize.

Bring the student to the front of the class and hand her an actual dollar while the class applauds. If you are uneasy with using actual money as the reward, you can substitute other items. However, it must be something that the students all recognize as having real value—play money, for example, that students can cash in for a prize from the class prize box.

Post-Activity Review and Discussion

If your experience with "Dollars for Details" is similar to mine, you will find that even the poorest writers in your class quickly pick up the look and nature of effective details—and begin to incorporate them into their writing. I have found this to be the single most effective tool in upgrading the general quality of a class's written details—all for the cost of three or four dollars a week.

Workout #19: Where Nothing Happens . . .

Quick Summary & Purpose

** **Purpose:** • Learn what does—and what does not—create story excitement.

Summary: This is a fun writing assignment that forces students to make something ordinary and mundane still seem to be exciting to the reader. Once this concept and writing technique are learned, they work on and for all types of writing and for any and all writing assignments.

Key Grades

Excellent: 5th & 6th. Good: 4th.

Time Required

Introduction & Writing: 30 minutes

Review, Sharing & Discussion: 15 to 30 minutes

Introduction

All students long to make their stories (and other narratives) exciting. They crave the glory of producing something others call "exciting." Most, sadly, fail time and time again.

Why such pervasive and widespread failure? Simply put, it is because students ignore the writing elements that really do create excitement and try to force writing elements to create excitement that are not capable of accomplishing that grand feat.

First, what is excitement? It is a feeling, an emotion manifested in the mind of a reader. Excitement is actually a momentary expression of anticipatory tension. Excitement exists in close anticipation of an action and dissipates quickly after that action is completed.

Second, what *doesn't* create excitement? Action. The actions and events in a story cannot, will not, and never have—in and of themselves—created excitement. Most students believe that action does create excitement because they feel that excitement during action sequences. However, the excitement isn't created by the action. No. It is created by other writing elements that then come to fruition and are experienced during subsequent action events.

Third, what *does* create excitement? That question is the exact point of this workout. Of the Eight Essential Elements of effective narratives (see TIP #5), it is Risk and Danger that create the feeling we call excitement. If nothing can go wrong, if story characters anticipate no conflicts or risks, then readers will feel no excitement.

From *Writing Workouts to Develop Common Core Writing Skills: Step-by-Step Exercises, Activities, and Tips for Student Success, Grades 2–6* by Kendall Haven. Santa Barbara, CA: Libraries Unlimited. Copyright © 2015.

Directions

Tell the class that they are going to write a personal essay based on this prompt:

You're walking home from school, and on that walk absolutely nothing exciting happens. It's just a walk to home during which nothing unusual, or in any way out of the ordinary, happens. Write an essay describing this walk to home . . . and make your essay exciting to read.

Note: Two common alternatives in these directions:

1. **Use some other common starting point than school.**

2. **Substitute "riding the school bus" for "walking." However, even though many do ride the school bus each day, walking provides more fodder for story material than do the confines of a school bus.**

The Rules

1. Students must use actual streets, buildings, and places they would normally see on their walk home.

2. They will write this as a first draft (double space), but should not worry about editing or spell checking during this writing period

3. They MUST make their essay exciting. Most students (if not all) will instantly object and argue that if nothing exciting *happens*, they won't be able to write an exciting essay. You should respond by saying, *"The rules stand, nothing exciting can actually happen during the walk but, yes, you can make the essay you write exciting."* Let them struggle with that seeming contradiction. However, it isn't a contradiction at all, and during the post-writing discussion, you will be able to use their writing to clearly demonstrate what makes writing exciting.

Post-Activity Review and Discussion

Collect the essays and evaluate them overnight. Many (often most) will try to sneak "exciting" action into their essay. Cross it out in bold red marker. Look for those who have kept to the rules.

In class, lead a discussion about what creates narrative excitement. If the readers perceive that real risk and danger exist for a character, whatever that character does will be exciting.

Example: *Walking up the front steps to the porch of your house is not exciting. But what if the reader knows that a pressure-sensitive bomb has been placed under the third step? The person walks up the curving walkway and steps up onto the first step. He steps up onto the second step. A car horn honk makes him turn around and step back one step as he waves at a passing neighbor. He steps back up on the second step. He lifts his foot to step again . . . but pauses as his barking dog romps around the corner of the house, tail wagging. He turns back toward the house and lifts his foot to step up onto the third step. . . . But suddenly remembers that he has to roll the trash cans back up the driveway since the garbage truck emptied them today. . . . See how imminent risk and danger create the excitement?*

However, if nothing out of the ordinary happens, if there are no secretly planted bombs, how can a writer create excitement? By creating risk and danger **in the mind of their character**. The best source of excitement is to let readers see into the mind (thinking) of a character. Their worries, fears, anxieties create the excitement readers need.

Example: *I walk along the sidewalk of 3rd Street next to that row of storefronts between Jones and Montague. A dog on the other side of the street is. . .is watching me . . . A big dog . . . I think a Doberman. . . . I think he's glaring at me. . . . And he's not on a leash! At any moment he'll pull back his lips and growl. I'll see yellow, blood-stained killer teeth. He could dash over here in three seconds! He'll rip me apart! And I'm trapped against these lousy storefronts. All the doors are locked. Why do the stores all have to close up at 5:00 PM? I'm trapped out here to die all alone torn into a thousand shreds by a vicious yellow-eyed killer. . . . Wait. He's not opening his mouth to bare his fangs. Just to lick his master's hand. . . . And look! He is on a leash. I hadn't noticed it before. It's black like the dog. . . . They're walking off down the street . . . I . . . I get to live!*

This brings up the second teaching point of this exercise (see TIP #8). To allow readers inside the mind of a character, writers must think in TFSS terms. (TFSS stands both for the mnemonic "Thursday, Friday, Saturday, Sunday" and for the key internal character information "Think, Feel, Sense, Say."—what a character thinks, how he feels, how he senses (perceives) the scenes around him, and what he says.) It is through these bits of moment-by-moment internal character information that readers become aware of that internal character world that creates true story excitement.

Use as many student examples from student essays as you can of sentences and even phrases that delve into this internal character world. Allow other students to react and to reflect on the two key concepts of this exercise: risk and danger, and the internal character musings revealed through TFSS—both the keys to narrative excitement.

As a final option, have students rewrite their essays based on what they learned from the class discussion. Read and compare the two essay versions, and then file these revised essays in their student writing folders.

Workout #20: I Love It; I Hate It!

Quick Summary & Purpose

** **Purpose:** • Learn the role of a character's thoughts and reactions in creating voice and revealing character personality.

Summary: This is another workout in refining student mastery of voice. This time, however, student writers will focus not on the actual words a character says, but on how the character reacts to, and thinks about, events and situations.

Key Grades

Excellent: 4th, 5th, & 6th. Very good: 3rd.

Time Required

Writing: 30 minutes

Review & Discussion: 15 to 20 minutes

Introduction

What does it mean to have a *voice*? What makes one voice different from another? Discuss this as a class before you proceed.

"Voice" refers to a combination of two things: **what** people say and **how** they say it. The vocabulary characters use (big words, monosyllabic utterances, lots of adjectives, no modifiers, the word "like" or "basically" in every sentence, etc.) and how they phrase and construct what they say (short, choppy sentences; long run-together sentences, etc.) are aspects of what characters say.

Volume, tone, pitch, breathiness, speed, etc.—these are all aspects of how characters say what they say.

Combine those two and you have a voice.

Question: How do student writers create unique, specific, interesting voices for their characters? Decide what a character would say and wouldn't say—as well as what the character would and wouldn't think. Then decide on the character's emotional state—how he feels. Let that emotion dictate how the character says what he says.

This fun writing workout will clearly demonstrate both the techniques and the allure of effective character voices.

From *Writing Workouts to Develop Common Core Writing Skills: Step-by-Step Exercises, Activities, and Tips for Student Success, Grades 2–6* by Kendall Haven. Santa Barbara, CA: Libraries Unlimited. Copyright © 2015.

Directions

Students will write two half-page descriptive stories, one at a time, each on its own piece of paper. These will be first-person stories. The student writer him- or herself will be the main character.

The first story will describe a typical, ordinary, everyday walk home from school (or other agreed-upon starting point). All of the places, sights, sounds, and occurrences in each story must be real, actual places and typical events and happenings.

While writing this first story, students will pretend that this walk is their favoritest thing to do in all the world. Pick specific (S-P-E-C-I-F-I-C) details along the walk, and show how the writer reacts to, and thinks/feels about, them.

The writer's job is to make it clear to readers of this paragraph that the writer *loves* this walk. Show us *exactly* what the student does on this walk, and make us know that this is the greatest, and most fun, thing he or she can imagine doing.

Give students 15 minutes to write.

Stop the writing and tell students that they will now rewrite their description of their walk home. In this second version, they MUST do exactly the same things, in the same order, and have exactly the same experiences as in the first paragraph. However, this time, they must write it so that it is clear to readers that the student loathes, hates, and despises this walk more than anything else he or she can imagine.

Same walk. Same sights, sounds, and actions. But opposite feelings and reactions.

How will they communicate the difference? Through the voice (in this case the thoughts and reactions) of the writer.

Post-Activity Review and Discussion

Collect all papers and review their writing. Look for students who have created two clear personalities and viewpoints in their two paragraphs. Have several of these students read both paragraphs to the class.

As a class, discuss what specific language creates a sense of both the scene and the character. What language stayed the same? What changed? What was the effect of the changes? How does each paragraph build an expectation in your mind of what the character would do and say in other situations and settings?

Workout #21: The Best Field Trip

Quick Summary & Purpose

** **Purpose:** • Create an opportunity for a persuasive essay for which students feel genuine passion and in which they have a possible vested interest.

Summary: Students will focus on the use of sensory details to enhance a persuasive argument by creating and controlling the specific vivid images readers mentally build.

Key Grades

Excellent: All intermediate grades

Time Required

30 to 40 minutes for writing. (I recommend that you allow students to take their written version home to edit, revise, and expand overnight.)

In-class sharing is optional but valuable since it gives you a chance to demonstrate what makes a written piece persuasive.

Introduction

Everyone loves field trips. In most schools, students bubble over with ideas for field trips the class should take. There are typically almost as many ideas for a class trip as there are students to partake in the trip. This means that your students are loaded with energy and passion on this topic. In this workout, you'll use that reservoir of focused energy to launch and refine their persuasive writing.

Directions

Build up and preface the assignment any way you like. The assignment is simple:

Students will describe a field trip they want the class to take.

Rules: The sky is the limit. No money worries or limits. BUT each student must describe the trip in detail (in *vivid* D-E-T-A-I-L), say why he or she thinks it would be a good trip for the class to take, and prove that it fits with the educational goals of the class and school. You may impose any other limits on the choice of field trip that feel right to you.

Their goal is to write their description so compellingly and alluringly that they persuade every student in class to vote for their trip.

Collect and review their trip descriptions. Grade them if you must. However, I think it is far more important to identify essays (or parts of essays) that are particularly effective (vivid description, create a you-are-there feeling, make a compelling case, etc.). Flag these to share with the class.

Post-Activity Review and Discussion

Have student writers read the flagged portions of their essays to the class. Discuss what makes this writing effective and persuasive.

As a fun option, allow students to read their essays before having the class vote on the trip they most want to take. After the vote, discuss why the winning essay persuaded students to vote for it.

Workout #22: Let the Jury Decide

Quick Summary & Purpose

** **Purpose:** • Teach deeper story comprehension skills.
- Develop a better sense of, and appreciation for, the power of character motive as a determinant of reader reaction to, and feelings about, both the character and the story.

Summary: There is no better way to decide if a character's actions were right or wrong, justified or unjustified, than to hold a courtroom trial where students can present the arguments pro and con and debate the issue. Students love the courtroom drama and get a valuable opportunity to evaluate complex character behavior and its relationship to the students' own world.

Key Grades

Excellent: 4th, 5th, & 6th

Time Required

To organize and assign roles: 20 to 30 minutes

Student planning time: 3 to 4 days elapsed time with no specific classroom time devoted to their work

Actual trial: 30 to 60 minutes

Post-activity Discussion: 20 minutes

Introduction

It is always clear whether or not a story character did it or didn't do it. The story text tells us. However, major questions often linger over whether or not that character was justified (morally or ethically) to do what he or she did—about whether he or she was "right" or "wrong" to do it. That analysis requires a deeper level of story analysis and tends to focus on character motive. That question is also the focus of this workout.

Directions

Pick a story and read it with the class. Best if the story is both familiar and short (folk tales are typically ideal). Pick a story in which characters do things that are technically a crime: "The Big Bad Wolf" (property destruction), "Goldilocks" (breaking and entering), "Wile E. Coyote" (attempted murder), etc.

From *Writing Workouts to Develop Common Core Writing Skills: Step-by-Step Exercises, Activities, and Tips for Student Success, Grades 2–6* by Kendall Haven. Santa Barbara, CA: Libraries Unlimited. Copyright © 2015.

You decide on the most appropriate character to "arrest" and charge with ***morally unjustifiable actions***. Notice that you will not hold court to decide if the character "did it." That has already been established by the factual statements of the story. The trial will determine whether or not that character was justified in doing what he or she did. With only rare exception, this will be either the main character or the antagonist.

Announce to the class that they will hold a formal courtroom trial to judge the actions of this character and decide if the character you have chosen was justified or not. The class must agree on the specifics of the charges (which exact actions were unjustifiable and wrong). Reemphasize that the charge is not guilt or innocence (that's a factual question that was answered by story information), but were they *justified* in doing it (a moral and ethical question for students to debate).

Now pick students and appoint them as the principal positions for the trial. Pre-appoint the following positions:

1. **Judge.** The judge is responsible for procedural matters (allowing questions to be asked, handling objections, allowing witnesses to be called, etc.) and ensuring that no direct story information is contradicted by any witness. (In some classrooms the teacher holds this position.)

2. **Prosecutor(s).** Prosecutors must identify all information in the story that tends to incriminate the defendant (show that the defendant's actions are not justifiable) and to identify the story witnesses who could best report that information during the trial. Witnesses need not have appeared in the actual story, but must have a strong reason to know firsthand the information they will report. Additional background and character witnesses may also be created and called.

   I usually appoint a lead prosecutor and three assistants to help research, strategize, develop the prosecution case, and to help write questions for different witnesses.

3. **Defense Counsel(s).** Defense counsel must prepare *for* the defendant what the prosecutor is trying to prepare *against* the defendant.

   Again, I typically appoint a lead attorney and three assistants.

4. **Defendant.** The defendant must be thoroughly familiar with the story and prepare, with defense counsel, explanations to rationalize and justify his or her reported story actions.

Other witnesses will be selected from the class membership as needed by either team of lawyers. The rest of the class will act as jury.

Allow two or three days for each team of lawyers to build their case and decide on a list of witnesses. (Many will not have appeared in the original story but will either be outside character witnesses or unreported witnesses to story events.) Witness lists must then be submitted to the judge and approved by both the judge and you. You will probably want to limit the number of witnesses each side may call.

If each team calls four witnesses, 17 students will have active roles in the actual trial. In smaller classes, you will only have a few students left to form the jury pool.

Because little classroom time is blocked out for trial prep work, many teachers give no assignment to those serving as the jury. Others assign the jury pool to research court proceedings and the responsibilities of each major player.

Regularly consult with the two teams of attorneys to make sure that they each have a good story line for their case and have developed it sufficiently to have specific witnesses and a list of specific questions for each. Encourage them to think creatively in what they will try to prove in court and in how they will solicit the needed information from witnesses.

Lawyers may definitely bring in information, witnesses, ideas that are not in the original story. Help them make the trial fun for the class as well as instructive about the power of motives. Help the lawyer teams explore the motives of the defendant and also how they will bring that information into the trial.

Even if you have appointed a student judge, you will serve as the story defendant: overrule anything that factually violates the story.

Assign the role of approved witness to different students who should have enough time to review the story and decide what they would and wouldn't logically know, how they feel about story events, and to infer any history they need to explain their position and their interpretation of story events. Witnesses (in collaboration with the lawyer team that will bring them into court) are free to add anything not directly covered in the story. But they cannot contradict the actual, stated story without your express permission.

On the day of the trial, physically set up the classroom as a courtroom. The judge can swear witnesses before they testify. Hold the trial: defense case first; prosecution second. Don't have the jury deliberate after the trial. Simply have them vote to see who won.

Post-Activity Review and Discussion

Good stories often place characters in the kind of jeopardy that requires them to make shaky moral and ethical decisions. This is the perfect fodder for a character trial.

There is no factual issue at stake in the trial. Story information establishes the guilt of the defendant. Being justified in a technically illegal act, however, is a moral and ethical question. These questions require us to know the defendant better, to understand his or her motives and feelings.

At the end of the trial, regardless of the outcome, the story and story characters will be more interesting and more important to your students. Character information creates a sense of closeness. The more often students experience that concept, the more likely they are to fully develop the characters they tell or write about.

Workout #23: The Detail Game

Quick Summary & Purpose

** **Purpose:** • Develop the ability to identify and form effective, imaginative descriptive detail.

Summary: Students will use only direct sensory detail to describe an object for their team that team members cannot actually see. In so doing, students must develop a better sense of the range and form of effective sensory details.

Key Grades

Excellent for all intermediate grades

Time Required

15 to 20 minutes

Introduction

Games and contests are always fun. This is a workout constructed in the form of a competitive game. The student who is "It" on a team must use only direct sensory detail to successfully describe an object for his or her team.

Directions

Divide the class into two teams. The exercise is played as a contest between these two groups. Have one student (the Contestant) from one team step out of sight of the other students. Give the Contestant an object that they must describe well enough for their team members to guess what it is. Start with simple objects such as a book, a pencil, an eraser, paper clips, an orange, a cardboard box, a glass, a paper cup, etc. Even those will be hard enough.

While describing this object for their team, the Contestant may not use the word itself or a synonym for it. He must physically *describe* the object, not classify it. They may not use hierarchical categories. If it's a pencil, they couldn't say "a #2" or "a writing instrument." If it's an orange, they couldn't say "fruit." If it's a brick, they couldn't say "construction material." Those are all classification categories that either contain or are contained in the word, not descriptions.

Neither may students provide clues about the history of the object or about its function—what you do with the object. For this game, students must use only direct sensory observation and description.

What might they say? For pencil: "Long, yellow, hexagonal, pink rubber at one end. Pointed black lead at the other." For orange: "Spherical, the size of your fist. Bumpy skin. Skin tastes bitter. Inside it's sweet and juicy. Smells perfume-y." And so on.

Give the Contestant a very limited time (5 to 10 seconds) to think of what description he or she will use before beginning. Limit the number of guesses by the team to avoid rapid-fire wild guessing of anything that might fit with the first descriptive clue. Three or four guesses should be plenty for guessing each object.

Any time the Contestant gives an illegal clue (saying, for example, that an orange is round and colored orange), he forfeits his turn. His team gets no points, and the game moves to the next Contestant from the other team.

You may want to pause and discuss as a class what other details might have been used that would have more quickly and successfully led the team to a correct guess. It is valuable for students to see what effective detail looks like.

Shift to a student on the other team who describes the next object for her team to guess. The game element comes from the contest you set up between the two teams. Each describer has a goal. The contest is to see which team meets that goal best when it is their turn. I have seen four goals used that all work well. Advance through these four as your students are ready for them.

1. Time. Each Contestant tries to get his or her team to correctly identify the object as fast as possible. Score is measured in seconds. Low score wins. Students stopped for illegal clues get the maximum allowable time (30 seconds, for example).

2. Efficiency. Successfully describe an object in as few *words* as possible within a fixed amount of time. (Thirty seconds is usually adequate.) A team's score is the actual number of words the Contestant used in his or her description. Low score wins.

3. Non-Visual. Each Contestant's description may only use senses other than sight (smell, feel, taste, sound). The goal may be for either minimum time or minimum number of words. Score is measured in either seconds or words. Low score wins.

4. Referral. Contestant descriptions may only use similes and metaphors. (For example, a Contestant might describe an orange as "Round as the earth itself. Sweet as a welcome bird's song. The color of a glowing, morning sun just peeking over the horizon.") The goal is minimum time. Score is measured in seconds. Low score wins.

Alternate Version

I have often used an alternate version of this game. At their seats, students secretly pick out one physical object in the classroom. They then describe, in writing, that object.

They may not name the object or say what it is. However, they may include in their description:

*   **Sensory information** (what you'd get from your own senses if you could see, hear, touch, smell, and taste the object)
*   **Function** (what the object does or what you do with it)

- **Likenesses** (what it reminds you of; similes and metaphors to compare this object with others)
- **History** (where it came from; what has happened to it in the past)

One student reads his or her description—one bit of description at a time with extended pauses between each. The class visually searches the room trying to figure out which object is being described.

After an object has been correctly identified, discuss which kinds of descriptive information were the most helpful in identifying that object. Also solicit ideas from the class of alternate descriptive wording the volunteer student could have used that would have more quickly led to identifying the object.

Post-Activity Review and Discussion

Good description creates specific, memorable, unique images in readers' minds. A writer doesn't have to describe all of an object, just those unique and key aspects or features that fix and specify a picture of the thing being described. Good description should involve more than just the sense of sight. Often detail for other senses is more powerful and informative. Have students look for opportunities for vivid description when they write and edit, and then search for unique, specific, imaginative descriptions for those places, characters, and events.

Quick Summary & Purpose

** **Purpose:** • Students learn to more fully envision the world through the eyes of another being (to empathize).

• Students develop the ability to create more fully developed and rounded characters.

Summary: Students will write a story describing a day-in-the-life of themselves as a chosen animal. The real value comes in making students more fully consider and develop this animal and all of the aspects of its daily existence.

Key Grades

Good for all intermediate grades

Time Required

Prep and planning: 15 minutes

Writing: 30 to 45 minutes

Introduction

The goal of this workout is to help students learn to put themselves more fully and realistically in the place of another. Everyone has a favorite animal. Most children have imagined being that animal and have fantasized about what they could and would do. This workout lets them take that imagining one big step further.

Directions

Students will each write a story. To do that, they must each pick the one animal they would most want to be.

After they have picked their animal, their assignment is to describe one day in the life of that animal.

"Animal Me" Planning Questions

As you plan your story about one day in your life as an animal, decide how and where to include answers to these questions:

- What animal would you most like to be?
- Why would you want to be *that* animal?
- What would you do?
- What would you be able to do that you can't do now?
- What would you fear?
- What would you have to avoid?
- What would be the hardest and easiest parts/aspects of your life as that animal?
- What would you need?
- How would you get it?
- How would you stay safe?

Before they start to write, use this guided oral exercise as a planning activity.

Put students into groups of three. For one minute (you time it), student #1 will describe the animal he chose, focusing on all of the qualities he likes and admire about this animal. Student #1's goal is to make the other two students wish that they had also chosen this animal as their animal.

At one minute, you call, "Stop!" Then for 45 seconds the other two students can ask any question about that animal or that relates to that animal. Student #1 must answer all questions—even if he has to make up an answer. The student may not say, "I don't know," or "It doesn't matter." The student must provide or create an answer for every question.

After 45 seconds, switch to student #2. This exercise takes just over five minutes.

Have students switch groups so that everyone is with two new people. Repeat the exercise. Except, this time, students will use their one minute to describe all of the dangers their animal could face and all of the things that could reasonably go wrong during the day they will describe.

In less than 15 minutes (total time) an amazing amount of story planning has taken place. Each student has both developed his or her own character and story, but has also listened to (and gotten new ideas from) four other students.

Some teachers now allow a short research period so that students can look up real answers to questions they were asked for which they did not have a good answer.

Now they write. Either project the list of questions for them to see, or make a copy for student to have right there at their desks.

This writing is another excellent candidate for a formal round of revision before editing and submission. Set the stories aside for a day. Then take them back out and have students make sure that they actually did answer each of the questions. They can add or reorder information as needed.

During this revision, students should assess whether or not they have crafted a good story. Does it flow logically and swiftly? Does it make sense? Are there enough details to create the vivid images readers need? Is the story exciting? Have they built suspense and tension? Have they sufficiently developed and presented their animal character so that every reader will be able to view the world through this character's eyes?

Post-Activity Review and Discussion

No formal post-activity discussion is needed. It is valuable to allow students to hear what others wrote. Still, the key learning comes from the doing—from struggling to fully describe the world through the eyes of another being.

Workout #25: Random Stories

Quick Summary & Purpose

** **Purpose:** • This is a fun, creative, energizing writing workout.

Summary: Students will have only a fixed amount of time to create a story that links four randomly selected pieces of story information.

Key Grades

Excellent for all intermediate grades

Time Required

10 minutes to pick objects and to plan

15 minutes to write

15 minutes to share

Introduction

For many (if not most) students, the hardest part of writing is getting an idea for what to write about. It is always difficult to start a story when it can be about anything. Better to help students focus in on something—anything—specific. Get that initial idea, and it instantly sparks the images and events of the accompanying story. This workout is a fun way to get all students past those whiny "I don't know what to write about . . ." blues and spark their energy and eagerness to write.

Directions

Have two students each name a random object. (You have veto power if you think their choice is inappropriate). Keep it simple and reasonably generic (a ripped glove, a bent spoon, a deflated football, a cracked skateboard, etc.). Write these on the board. Have a third student pick a place (a story setting). Again, best to stay generic in their choice (a cave, the beach, a city park, a living room, a subway platform, the bottom of the ocean, etc.). Write this setting on the board.

A fourth student picks a weather condition (rain, sleet, hot sunshine, fog, etc.). This also goes on the board.

The final (fifth) student identifies a character by defining these four character traits: species, gender, age, and name. This information also goes on the board.

From *Writing Workouts to Develop Common Core Writing Skills: Step-by-Step Exercises, Activities, and Tips for Student Success, Grades 2–6* by Kendall Haven. Santa Barbara, CA: Libraries Unlimited. Copyright © 2015.

You want this workout to be valuable as well as fun. To do that, give students this writing assignment:

You will each write a story in 15 minutes that connects and incorporates these two objects, this setting, this weather condition, and this character.

Before you begin to write:

1. Create your main character (also your viewpoint character), and create a goal and motive for that character.

2. Plan on making each of these five things we pre-picked important to your story.

3. Make your story *exciting*! (Excitement comes from establishing risk and danger, not through action.)

Give students 5 minutes for planning and for jotting notes. Then 15 to actually write.

Key goals for their writing are creativity and development of their main character and his/her story.

Post-Activity Review and Discussion

During follow-up discussions, have several students read their stories. Discuss by analyzing the Eight Essential Elements (see TIP #5, the Eight Essential Elements) and by assessing how able the students were in incorporating the assigned items as important parts of their stories.

You'll find that both the writing and the reviewing are engaging and delightful to students.

Workout #26: Inferring a Character

Quick Summary & Purpose

** **Purpose:** • Students will become more consciously aware of how, and to what extent, they subconsciously and automatically make a number of character inferences from scant story information. This is a critical awareness for effective narrative writing.

Summary: We all love to watch—and to laugh at—classic cartoons. However, all cartoons are strongly character based. They provide the perfect opportunity to explore how alluring characters are created and presented.

Key Grades

Excellent for all intermediate grades.

Time Required

45 minutes total

Introduction

Cartoons (especially the "Saturday morning classics") are always a delight to watch and to laugh at. They are also powerful character studies. It is that aspect of a cartoon that you will use in this workout to make your students more aware of the tools available to them—as writers—to develop and present their fiction and nonfiction characters.

Directions

Many of the old classic cartoons are available for free download on the Internet. My favorite for this workout are the Road Runner cartoons. My second favorite are Bugs Bunny cartoons that pit Bugs against Elmer Fudd.

Download a cartoon (let's assume you pick one of the Road Runner episodes) to your laptop, and use the computer projection system in your classroom to play the cartoon for your students.

They will certainly be engaged and pay attention.

In this cartoon there are two characters (the Road Runner and Wile E. Coyote, or Bugs and Elmer). Pick the villain to analyze during this workout.

Let students work in teams of two. They are to list everything they know and can infer from this cartoon about this character. I usually give them 15 minutes for this task.

As prompts, ask (or write on the board) the following areas for them to consider:

- Personality
- Physical abilities
- Mental abilities
- Dreams and goals
- Fears
- Flaws and disabilities
- Natural talents
- Strengths and weaknesses
- What I like about this character
- What I dislike about this character

Post-Activity Review and Discussion

Have individual teams read their lists. Discuss and refine as a class as you build a master list on the board. Once a good master list of character traits exists on the board, redirect the discussion to this question:

How did you decide that (the character) exhibits this trait?

That question takes students back to the source material. As they tear apart the original, they will uncover techniques that they each can use to increase the allure and appeal of their own characters.

Workout #27: Progressive Stories

Quick Summary & Purpose

** **Purpose:** • Reinforce student awareness of the essential structural elements of effective stories.

Summary: This is the first in a series of quick, in-class story development workouts that develop student confidence in their use of, and mastery of, the Eight Essential Elements of effective narrative writing.

Key Grades

Excellent for all intermediate grades

Time Required

Varies from 5 minutes to 20 minutes

Introduction

Progressive stories are stories where one person makes up a short part and then passes the story to the next person to make up a bit more. Everyone thinks that this will be fun. In truth, most students become quickly bored and disengage from the emerging story. Why? Because the stories are inevitably boring.

There are, however, ways to control and shape these stories by the rules you use for their creation that will keep everyone riveted. That is the idea behind this writing workout.

Directions

There are three options for creating effective student progressive stories that I want to offer. All can be both fun and productive.

In-Class Progressive Stories

These are stories that the class invents on the fly. Student #1 starts the story and tells (your option) one sentence or for a set number of seconds (usually 15 to 20). Then the story passes to student #2.

While these are fun for students, there are several red-flag dangers. First, the stories quickly become illogical and meaningless. All students (except for that one student who makes up the next part) tune out and are bored. Second, the stories don't demonstrate anything about the structure of effective stories to students.

From Writing Workouts to Develop Common Core Writing Skills: Step-by-Step Exercises, Activities, and Tips for Student Success, Grades 2–6 by Kendall Haven. Santa Barbara, CA: Libraries Unlimited. Copyright © 2015.

If you try this, I recommend that you add in a proviso: after each person supplies her part to the story, the class must vote (thumbs up or thumbs down) to accept it. You will instruct the class that their vote must be based on whether or not this newly added part makes sense and actually advances the story as it has developed to this point.

If the class rejects a student's offering, that student has one chance to revise her input. If their offering fails a second time, that student is skipped and the story passes to the next student.

To make this format more interesting, and to keep all students locked into the story, make the progression around the class random. That way students do not know if they will be the next teller, and all must prepare for that eventuality with each new teller.

Post-Activity Review and Discussion

No post-activity discussion is necessary. Do it as a fun activity, and move on with the day. The learning comes from how students plan and ponder their contributions to each progressive story.

Workout #28: 30-Second Story

Quick Summary & Purpose

** **Purpose:** • Reinforce student awareness of the essential structural elements of effective stories.

Summary: This is another in the series of quick, in-class story development workouts that develop student confidence in their use of, and mastery of, the Eight Essential Elements of effective narrative writing.

Key Grades

Excellent for all intermediate grades

Time Required

15 minutes

Introduction

This is a VAST improvement on the more general class progressive story. It is a bit more challenging for the selected students. But it is vastly more instructive and productive. Ultimately, your students will find this game format far more fun and will want to be volunteered as their story development and understanding skills improve.

Directions

Bring four students to the front of the room and tell them that they are going to make up a four-minute story, 30 seconds at a time. While this is a verbal exercise, it focuses on aspects of story creation, structure, and development.

One student starts the story and tells it for 30 seconds. Then the second, third, and fourth tellers each tell for 30 seconds. Now the first teller invents and tells the story for a second 30 seconds, and so forth to the fourth teller's second turn, during which time the story must be ended. You time each segment, calling, "Switch!" at the 30-second break points. There are no pauses for thought between tellers. The second one ends, the next begins, even if the story is in the middle of a sentence.

The *General Rules* keep this story from degenerating into a mindless, boring story, as are most circle stories. The *Special Requirements* focus the class on that aspect of story you want them to work on.

General Rules

These six rules apply every time your class uses the 30-Second Story exercise. They should be considered a mandatory part of this exercise since they force the four students to create a single, unified story.

1. The first student starts the story by providing three key story elements during his or her first 30-second telling: identity of the main character, that character's goal during the story (what he or she wants to do or get), and an initial setting for the story.

2. The second teller, during his or her first 30-second telling, must create at least one suitable obstacle that blocks the main character from the goal. If the first teller provided one obstacle, the second provides a second obstacle.

3. Every teller must accept the first teller's main character and goal and use them as the focus and purpose for each story segment.

4. Every teller must pick up the story *exactly* where the previous teller stopped with no temporal or spatial jumps. They may not shift to other characters, other settings, or other events at the beginning of their 30-second period.

5. Any teller may resolve an obstacle, but must immediately pose another one to take its place, so that there is always at least one obstacle on the table for the character to struggle against. And,

6. The final teller must bring the story (goal of the main character) to some resolution during his or her final 30-second telling.

The class should track and evaluate each of the four students' success with the General Rules. This task helps every student recognize and appreciate the role of goal, conflict, and struggles in basic story structure.

Special Requirements

In addition to the *General Rules*, you will create **Special Requirements** for each telling. **Special Requirements** apply only to the current round of the 30-Second Story. After meeting these requirements under the pressure of a timed, improvised story in front of the class, students will find it easy to consider that facet of story writing in the future. You select the **Special Requirements** to emphasize and focus on any aspect of story writing you want the class to study.

Some commonly used **Special Requirements** are:

- **Character Development.** Require that each teller reveal two new bits of significant information about the main character's history, likes, fears, physical presence, personality, activity, etc. during each of his or her two 30-second telling periods.

- **Senses.** We often describe only what we see. Richer stories come from engaging more of the listener's senses. Require that each teller include detailed information about three, four, or all five senses during each 30-second telling.

- **Action Verbs.** Verbs of state (verbs such as is, are, was, am, were, etc. that only indicate a state of being) do little to fire a listener's imagination and create vivid, detailed mental images. Require that each teller use no more than two—or even one—verb of state in each telling.

    These verbs of state are often used as "helper" verbs. (He is going, or she was sitting.) Still, they always pull energy out of the text compared to the simple tenses. (He goes. She sat.) Have the class keep track.

- **Passive Voice.** Using passive voice is another way to suck energy and excitement out of a text. ("The chair was placed at the table," as opposed to "Dave placed the chair at the table." "The data were shown to be significant," as opposed to "Sharon showed that the data were significant.") For that reason, there are times when it is useful. However, passive voice is (generally) overused, and used at many of the wrong places. Require that students use NO passive voice in any of their 30-second telling periods.

- **Descriptive Detail**. We all drop modifiers and write (or speak) in simple subject-verb sentences when we're not sure of what we're writing about. Hand each teller a slip of paper on which you have written an object with several appropriate modifiers (e.g., a long red string, or an empty brown bottle). Each teller will thus have his or her own object. During each of their two 30-second telling periods, each teller must include that object with its modifiers in the story. The class's job is to detect what was written on each teller's paper. Each teller's job is to keep the class from successfully identifying the object. Tellers can succeed only by peppering their 30-second telling with other modifiers, thus disguising the ones assigned to them. Soon, searching for descriptive modifiers will be automatic.

- **Scene Description.** Young story writers often forget that, just because they can see each scene in their heads, readers cannot also see those scenes. Require that each teller spend half of his or her 30-second periods describing details of the scenes of the story.

Similarly, characterization, simile and metaphor, word choices, irony, or any other facet of story writing can become the Special Requirement focus of a 30-Second Story. As your students become more adept at the form of this exercise, you can give them two or three Special Requirements to accomplish during each telling session in addition to the General Rules.

Discuss with the class as a whole the four tellers' success with both General Rules and Special Requirements. Then discuss the effective use of, and importance of, the Special Requirements aspect of story construction. Finally, have a second group of four create a second story with the same Special Requirements. Have the class compare and contrast these two groups looking for improvement in the Special Requirements area.

In 20 minutes, two groups can create different stories while focusing on the *Special Requirement* of the day, and the whole class will have watched and discussed that aspect of story writing in some detail. If used only once a week, this technique will greatly expand your class's mastery of successful story structure.

Remember that making up a story under pressure, in front of peers, is much scarier than One-on-One-on-One-on-Ones or most other story-development exercises. Introduce the 30-Second

Story without *Special Requirements*. Then gradually build into more complex requirements always keeping the tone that of a light-hearted game.

Options/Variations

Many teachers have found that their class responds more enthusiastically when a system of award points is created for the game. Tellers get points for successfully meeting General and Special Requirements. Class members get points for noting discrepancies or for accurately tracking certain aspects of the Special Requirements. The race for points is on, and the class is hooked. They all want to be selected to the four-person story-creating team because tellers build more points. The audience studies every word, looking for their share of the points. These points can then go toward whatever system of prizes and rewards you use.

Post-Activity Review and Discussion

No post-activity discussion is necessary. Do it as a fun activity and move on with the day. The learning comes from how students plan and ponder their contributions to each progressive story.

Workout #29: Written Progressives

Quick Summary & Purpose

** **Purpose:** • Reinforce student awareness of the essential structural elements of effective stories.

Summary: This is another in the series of quick, in-class story development workouts that develop student confidence in their use of, and mastery of, the Eight Essential Elements of effective narrative writing.

Key Grades

Excellent for all intermediate grades

Time Required

15 minutes

Introduction

In this version of the progressive story, student write their additions to each building story, rather than sharing them orally.

Directions

The general rules for a written progressive story are that each student will add to the story they receive for a fixed amount of time (generally 30 to 60 seconds) during each time period and then pass the story on to another student. Depending on the format you choose, you will have to allot some time for each new student to read the existing story before his or her writing time begins.

The general rules are:

1. Student must start his or her additions *exactly* where the previous student left the story.

2. No temporal ("and in 50 years . . .") or spatial ("and across the globe in Australia . . .") jumps are allowed.

3. Each student must keep the same main character goal that was initially established.

4. If a student solves a problem, he or she must replace it with another problem or conflict so that the next writer will have something given to him or her to write about.

I have tried two options for this version of the progressive story:

1. Two students pass their two stories back and forth between them, each adding a bit to the story on each pass.

    The advantage here is that each student is familiar with both stories and requires less reading time to be ready to write his or her next addition to it. If you allow each student to write for 30 seconds and to read for 30 seconds, he or she will always have plenty of time for the reading no matter how long the total story becomes.

    The one potential problem with this scheme is that strong disagreements often arise over the direction and development of one or both of the stories and the two students become frustrated.

2. Each story passes, student by student, around the room as each new student adds his or her contribution.

    Problem #1 with this scheme is that, after three or four students have written their parts to the story, you must allow longer and longer reading blocks before each new student begins to write. I generally start this reading time at 15 seconds and then add 10 to 15 seconds for each extra segment students must read and absorb before they write.

    It is also essential for this option to place additional requirements on each new writer. The first student must create a main character and a goal. The second must create a problem or conflict that blocks the main character from goal attainment. Each new student can only solve an existing problem if he or she also creates a new problem. Each new contributor must include one new bit of character information (trait) for others to use. . . . That sort of thing.

Post-Activity Review and Discussion

No post-activity discussion is necessary. Do it as a fun activity and move on with the day. The learning comes from how students plan and ponder their contributions to each progressive story.

Workout #30: Superheroes!

Quick Summary & Purpose

** **Purpose:** • Give students a chance to experience the elements that really make stories work for readers.

Summary: Students will each define themselves as a superhero, define their superpowers, and then develop a story about this superhero.

Key Grades

Good for all intermediate grades

Time Required

30 to 45 minutes for prep and planning

60 minutes for writing

Introduction

Every child dreams of being a superhero. Great! Use this energy and passion to encourage better writing. This writing workout focuses that energy on effective story writing.

Directions

The basic assignment is: "If you were going to be a superhero, describe what powers you would have and what you'd do with them." Let them write their superhero name and power.

However, don't allow students to start writing or even planning their story yet. Launch a class discussion along this line: without Kryptonite, Superman would be boring. Every superhero has a flaw, a weakness. What makes a superhero interesting? (Their fears, quirks, flaws, imperfections, and frailties.) What makes their stories exciting? (The amount of real risk and danger they face. That means that something or someone in the story must be capable of threatening— even overpowering—the superhero.)

Have all students write down what their superhero is afraid of, what defeats his or her power, what his or her character loves and hates. Also have students define their character's voice, quirks, flaws, and eccentricities.

Make sure each student does this before proceeding. Now define your superhero's arch villain. How can this villain defeat your superhero? What is something that you have to keep that villain from doing?

From *Writing Workouts to Develop Common Core Writing Skills: Step-by-Step Exercises, Activities, and Tips for Student Success, Grades 2–6* by Kendall Haven. Santa Barbara, CA: Libraries Unlimited. Copyright © 2015.

After—and only after—these things have been defined, students may proceed to writing their story about this superhero. Remember TIPS #5 and 8 as guides for their writing. Especially remember TIP #7: Think small. Encourage students to focus on a specific defined problem and not to try to "save the world."

Post-Activity Review and Discussion

No specific post-activity discussion is essential. It is always extremely beneficial for students to hear what others have written with the same instructions. I encourage creating a time for sharing. However, no other formal postmortem discussion is needed.

OTHER BOOKS OF WRITING ACTIVITIES AND GAMES

These are a few of the many good sources of writing and story muscle-building games and workouts.

Haven, Kendall. *Story Smart: Using the Science of Story to Persuade, Inspire, Influence, and Teach*. Santa Barbara, CA: Libraries Unlimited, 2014

Haven, Kendall. *Story Proof: The Science Behind the Startling Power of Story*. Westport, CT: Libraries Unlimited, 2009.

Haven, Kendall. *Get It Write! Creating Lifelong Writers from Expository to Narrative*. Portsmouth, NH: Teacher Ideas Press, 2004.

Haven, Kendall. *Super Simple Storytelling*. Englewood, CO: Teacher Ideas Press, 2000.

Haven, Kendall. *Write Right: Creative Writing Using Storytelling Techniques*. Englewood, CO: Teacher Ideas Press, 1999.

INDEX

ABOUT THE AUTHOR

KENDALL HAVEN is a master storyteller and author of 34 books who has conducted writing workshops at over 1,600 schools and has performed for total audiences of over 6.5 million. His published works include 24 books from Libraries Unlimited, including *Story Proof: The Science Behind the Startling Power of Story*; Story Smart: Using Story Science to Inspire, Persuade, Influence, and teach; *Get It Write! Creating Lifelong Writers from Expository to Narrative*; and *Write Right! Creative Writing Using Storytelling Techniques*.